HELMUT GOLLWITZER

The Rich Christians and Poor Lazarus

Translated by
DAVID CAIRNS

THE MACMILLAN COMPANY

To the students of Berlin
in gratitude for their insurgence
and insistent zeal

This book was originally published in German under the title "Die reichen Christen und der arme Lazarus"

The Macmillan Company
866 Third Avenue, New York, N.Y. 10022
Collier-Macmillan Canada Ltd., Toronto, Ontario

Library of Congress Catalog Card Number: 78–107048

First Printing

Printed in Great Britain
by D. J. Clark Ltd., Glasgow

CONTENTS

PREFACE

THIS book had its origin in the draft of a report to the Synod of the Protestant Church in Germany in October 1968. One of the tasks of the Synod was to receive the resolutions of the Uppsala Conference of the World Council of Churches (1968), and to give effect to them on a national level. I began writing immediately after my return from Uppsala; Uppsala had impressed on me the central importance of the responsibility of the Christian Church in the matter of a policy of development, in order to avert the threatening catastrophe of world hunger, which has already begun. And as I wrote, this book developed out of my sketch. Thus its first chapters still have the character of an address to the Synod—a character which I did not wish to eliminate by subsequent alterations. What I actually delivered to the Synod was a somewhat altered extract. I am conscious that this book raises more questions than it answers, and that it often enough suggests and asserts without adducing proofs. But its aim is not more than this, to make suggestions, and more should not be expected of it. I have been glad to make use of the Reports given by Johannes Hamel and Hans Thimme to the two Regional Synods of the United Evangelical Church in 1968, and of an unpublished study by H. E. Bosse-Hannover on Church Statements on the policy of development.

Just when I had completed my work of composition, Czechoslovakia was occupied by the armies of the five neighbouring states of the Warsaw Pact. What I said in this book about socialism and capitalism seemed to be discredited by this. What is really discredited is the socialism of the occupying states, a socialism which has got bogged down in hierarchical authoritarianism, and that is an occasion for plenty of criticism and self-criticism in all socialist groups, but no cause for resignation. Nor is it cause for believing that the socialist criticism of the capitalist system—a criticism which has been given even more point by the crisis in the policy of development—has been refuted. The Czechoslovakian renaissance was in effect a renaissance of socialism. This was the element of promise in it. Indignation about the Soviet occupation is hypocrisy, if it is expressed by those who once supported Hitler's occupations, or by those who find the American interventions in Vietnam and Santo Domingo and the blockade of Cuba to be in order. Today we have to listen to moral condemnations in the Security Council of the measures taken against Czechoslovakia, expressed by the representative of that same British government which—along with the Soviets—supports the Nigerian government by deliveries of arms, and which has declared a deadly hunger blockade of the Ibo people a legitimate method of war. Anyone who concerns himself with politics, as Uppsala has recently urged churchmen to do, will have to come to a clear and sober judgment about the barbarous state of mind of the majority of today's rulers—irrespective of the question whether they are atheists or agnostics, churchgoers and panegyrists of western and other civilizations. This state of mind may bring mankind to destruction. We must ask for its causes, and the possibilities of changing it.

This book is dedicated to the students of Berlin. By this I mean those who, among many thousands who attend the universities of West Berlin, are responsible for the fact that Berlin has for some time now been censured or praised as a place of unrest. I mean especially those of their spokesmen with whom in recent years I have come in contact, and who go in and out of my house. In contrast with many of my contemporaries and colleagues, who regard them with deep antipathy or at least shake their heads over them in bewilderment, I have come to love them for their sincerity, their courage, their feeling for freedom, their sense of responsibility for the future, and their dream of a more humane society. I have received from them encouragement, instruction, and the stimulus for new thought, and they, I hope, have benefited from some of the things that I and my friends have had to say in criticism and correction of them. This book does not deal with those matters, because this is not the place to pass judgment on their ideas and actions. I have merely mentioned their movement, because its manifestations might remind Christian congregations of similar possibilities of thought and action which cannot be strange to a group of people which has its point of gathering and mission in the gospel.

Among the students of whom I am thinking are young Christians, and others who have their difficulties with Christianity, churchgoers and those who do not go to church. But they have all made me conscious of an expectation that the Church and its message might still be relevant. Because this book would gladly confirm them in this expectation, and because at the same time there are many statements in it that could not have been written without their co-operation, it will be dedicated to them.

Berlin, Autumn 1968. HELMUT GOLLWITZER

1

THE POLITICAL CONSEQUENCES OF THE GOSPEL TODAY

We Are the Rich Man

WHO are we? Answer: We are the rich man. That is, incontestably, the most exact description of us. "We belong to that third of humanity which is concerned with slimming cures, while the other two-thirds are concerned with hunger". And this third consists for the most part of baptized Christians, the other two-thirds of unbaptized persons. So things have changed since the days when Paul made collections among the slaves in Corinth for the "poor" in Jerusalem. The baptized persons sit as rich men at a well-covered table, and poor unbaptized Lazarus lies outside at the door—really outside, and therefore even more powerless, easier to be passed over at our meal, than if he lay within our house, as the proletariat formerly did in our countries. "Christians rob Christians" was the title of a recent lecture by Helder Camara, the Archbishop of Recife, in Brazil,[1] in which he described the exploitation of the Latin American masses by North American capital and the indigenous upper classes; and we must write further that" baptized persons rob the unbaptized," when we consider the case of Asia and Africa.

Jesus' parable of the rich man and poor Lazarus (Luke 16: 19–31) tells how the baptized rich persons are repudiated by their Lord, and the baptized and unbaptized victims of exploitation are received into his bosom. "Inasmuch as ye did it not unto the least of these my brethren, ye did it not unto me."

"If they hear not Moses and the prophets, neither will they be persuaded, though one rose from the dead." One has risen from the dead, and the rich confess this at their table, and yet poor Lazarus, in millions, continues to hunger and to perish from hunger at their door. The point of this parable is not, as is often suspected, the consoling pipe-dream of heaven for poor Lazarus. It is addressed exclusively to the rich man. It is not meant to console the poor with the hope of recompense beyond the grave, but to warn the rich of damnation and to incite them to hear and act in this world. "The difference between the Christian hope of resurrection and a mythological hope is that the Christian hope sends a man back to his life on earth in a wholly new way which is even more sharply defined than it is in the Old Testament."[2] "We need not *ars moriendi*, the art of dying, but the resurrection of Christ to invigorate and cleanse the world today. *Here* is the answer to the saying, 'Give me where to stand and I will move the earth.' What a tremendous difference it would make if a few people really believed and acted upon that. To live in the light of the Resurrection, that is the meaning of Easter."[3]

In a pluralistic society we are tolerantly allowed to have every consolation that we can find for ourselves, even religious consolations, even those of Easter and eternal life. At the most we draw a little scorn on ourselves from those who take a pride in their enlightenment. But we bring on ourselves enmity and murder when we draw the consequences of these beliefs for this life, and place ourselves, like the late Martin Luther King at the head of the striking garbage collectors, as leaders of Lazarus' millions and really do what Uppsala resolved to bring about. Confessions of faith which do not have as their consequence far-reaching social changes in this world, are matters of private recreation, and therefore have long been tolerated as irrelevant and harmless. We shall only be able to make clear to our contemporaries the relevance of every article of our Confession of Faith, if we make clear its political and social revolutionary significance for society. "It is not a healthy sign when a congregation draws back in horror as soon as preaching becomes political—as if it could be unpolitical! A congregation which is conscious of its political responsibility will wish and request that preaching become political; they will understand it in a political sense, even if it does not use any of the terms of politics."[4] "The man who does not understand a proposition of *Church Dogmatics* in a political sense, has not yet understood it," said a Japanese professor of theology some time ago to his students about Karl Barth's work, and that is true of all good theology, and of every traditional dogma. Our theological discussion has—at least in part—been divided into a conservative insistence on the dogmatic tradition, and a liberal repudiation of the dogmatic content in exchange for an ethic of shared humanity. We are thus falling back into the worst tradition of the nineteenth century, in which conservative theologians were wont to be conservative in politics also, and the liberals believed themselves obliged to discard dogma in exchange for humanism. But this means tearing asunder things that belong together. Every article of the Confession of Faith has explosive and aggressive significance for the *status quo* of the old world, and an article that leaves our relationship to the other man and to society as it was, is not worthy to be an article of the Christian Faith.

Only by altered attitudes in this world, not by assertions about divine truths, which are claimed to be true "in themselves," can we bear witness to the relevance of our confession of faith. Therefore John A. T. Robinson is right to ask his question "Do we affirm the Easter faith in these days, when we insist that God raised Jesus from the dead—or when we dare to gamble our lives in the faith that God will raise us from the dead? Can we do the former, without doing the latter?"[5] And indeed, keeping our eye on the liberal reduction of faith to humanism, we shall also have to add, "Can we do the latter, without doing the former?"

Catholicity of the Church: Solidarity with Mankind

It repeatedly happens in the Church that some individual element is taken out of its context and treated as an end in itself. All individual elements in the Church have as their true context the work of Jesus Christ which is for the sake of the whole of humanity. This is the totality, the catholicity of the Church, which is described in the Report of Section I of Uppsala. There we read, "Since Christ lived, died and rose again for all mankind, catholicity is the opposite of all kinds of egoism and particularism."[6] Without doubt there was, and is, among us, an egoistic kind of piety, which is only interested in our own salvation, and in which the man Christ is made the servant of our own interests, instead of our being ourselves the servants of Christ's interests. Without doubt there is still among us a particularism of Christian groups and Confessions which has not yet been grasped by the Ecumenical Movement, and has not yet led beyond its own self-complacency, self-righteousness, and isolation. This is to be observed abroad in the young Churches, just as much as in the self-isolation of many of our congregations in relation to the congregations of other Confessions in the same place. Without doubt there is a self-centred pursuit of our academic theology, interested only in its scholarly perfection, and allergic to every reminder of theology's responsibility to the Church. It thus forgets the nature of Christian theology as *scientia practica* (the Protestant Fathers rightly compared it in this respect with medicine!), and forgets the unity of theory and practice, serving its own selfish whim instead of the whole cause of Jesus Christ.

All this is given the lie and judged by the simple and massive fact of world hunger. Poor Lazarus before our door is the living question why all this is happening, what benefit does he get from it all, whether all this is not impermissible frivolity. All these things place countless very practical hindrances in the way of realization of Church aid for development. All this is a luxury we can no longer allow ourselves.

This is what is implied by the Confession of the catholicity of the Church.

The Lord's Supper: Solidarity of the Fellowship

As there is only *one* baptism which incorporates us in the Body of Christ, so there is only *one* Lord's Supper and *one* Body of Christ. The question how can a body be eaten at the same time in many places, was rightly dismissed by our Lutheran Fathers as a foolish, fleshly, useless question, which understands nothing of God's promise. This is not an occasion for speculation, but a practical promise: you are, as a fellowship at the Lord's Table, *one* indivisible body with your Lord, and receive, in however many parts of the earth, the "Fellowship of the Body of Christ" (cf. 1 Cor. 10: 16–17). This has the practical consequence: "Those who have eaten the body of one Lord are looked on as one man." All the wars which Christians have waged against one another, all plundering of Christians by Christians, are sins against the fellowship of the Lord's Supper. The Lord's Supper stands as a judgment over the whole of church history. Does the Lord's Supper make us *one* fellowship? Then the misery of hungry Christians in other parts of the world is a misery within our fellowship, since geographical remoteness is irrelevant to the fellowship of faith. Here it becomes evident how particularistic our thinking still is, how national and geographical factors still weigh more with us than the confession of our faith. If there were here among us a crowd of starving people, it is to be hoped that we would not be able to build churches and church buildings of the expensive kind that we have become accustomed to build, until these members of the fellowship were at least saved from death by starvation! The Lord's Supper says: "Those who are starving out there, are also members of your fellowship! They are no further away from you than those who live in your parish." Thus every Communion has to do with development aid, and our whole church financial policy is confronted by the challenge directed to us by Uppsala to make "a visible sacrifice," by which terms at least five per cent. of the yearly income of our churches is indicated.[7]

Mission: Solidarity with non-Christians

Mission is Church in movement and we have learnt that today in the ecumenical movement. The Church is, by its very nature, missionary. This means, however, that it is permanently orientated towards those without, towards those who are not yet brothers, but should become brothers—and so, in a sense, are already brothers. That Christians rob and destroy Christians is bad enough, and a sin against the Lord's Supper. But that Christians rob and destroy non-Christians is no less evil, and a sin against baptism and mission, against the commission to make all peoples disciples and to batize them. As those for whose sake our Lord has dedicated himself and us to service, they stand no further from us than those who are already baptized.

The exhortation of the apostle, "Let us do good unto all men, especially unto them who are of the household of faith" (Gal. 6: 10), certainly does not mean that we should in the first place bother ourselves only about those who are likeminded with us, and only then, in the second place—and just as far as it is possible—bother about those who have other beliefs. No, what he means is, "Naturally you must begin with those with whom you live together in the fellowship, but then the boundaries of the fellowship must not be the boundaries of your loving activity; of course if there is a failure in philanthropy even within your fellowship, then your philanthropy to people outside it will not be worth much either." A Christendom that can sleep peacefully while fellow-Christians in other lands starve, and can go on building splendid churches, will not open its hands for hungry non-Christians either. But then it will have given the lie to its missionary activity.

Repentance: Solidarity in Colonial Guilt

An integral part of faith is *repentance*, the confession of our own guilt, and the relinquishing of our previous evil ways. We understand this often in too individualistic a manner, with reference only to our own actions. But my guilt includes also the guilt of my fathers, in so far as I unreflectingly continue in their ways and profit from them. We all profit from the colonial sins of our fathers, we reap their harvest—including also the fruits of hate—and one of the most decisive questions of development aid, is whether we are to break with this past, and make reparation for it, in so far as reparation is possible.

Thirty years ago there appeared a book with the title, *Europa*, which at that time was much read in the houses of protestant pastors and citizens. Because the Nazis were too extreme for the author, this book was considered to be in opposition to them, and because the author had made the journey from socialism to conservatism long before the rest of the German Socialist Party, it was reckoned as Christian. In this book by August Winnig[8] are to be found the sentences: "Here (in Europe) a wealth has been amassed, which exceeds every measure with which we are familiar. Nowhere at any previous time has such wealth accumulated upon the earth." Now, it is not true to say that it has "accumulated." It was a robbers' haul, the phenomenon of colonialism was one of its important causes, and without this cause the rise of Europe cannot be explained.

Here I am not considering the psychological and cultural results of the colonial epoch affecting the countries concerned. The profound self-estrangement out of which today "the torrent of our cries, full of shame, pain, and fury at this immense spiritual desolation within us,"[9] coming from these lands, sounds in our ears, and is often received by us with irritation and arrogance instead of understanding and acknowledgment of our guilt. Here ecumenical Christianity is confronted by a task of "spiritual revolutionary diakonia" which must provide food for thought for many, not only for those who are immediately involved in the missionary societies. Here I limit myself to the economic consequences.

The economy of the colonized countries was directed outwards and harnessed to the interests and needs of the colonizing powers. Therefore the industrial development of the colonized countries was hindered, and their educational systems were kept at the pre-technical stage. These countries were condemned to uniform cultures, and kept in complete economic servitude to the ruling power. Men and production were there merely to serve the rulers of the colony, and the colonial subject could daily see the rulers' prosperity and privileges, and by comparison his own deprivation of rights.[10] The older people among us will remember how much this was taken for granted by us. The news of colonial atrocities in the Congo and other places disturbed the white Christian community as little as did the protests of individual white Christians. The churches were indeed closely linked with white imperialism through the bond between missions and colonial politics. Besides Winnig's *Europa* there stood in many manses Hans Grimm's *Volk ohne Raum* (*People without Living Space*) in which, after the claim of the first sentence that bells should be tolled for this book (apparently our Church bells!), the expedition of Captain Erkert in German South West Africa was lauded as a feat of heroism. This was the man who drove the Hereros into the salt desert to die of hunger and thirst, just as today the Ibos in Biafra are being driven to die of hunger.

What the colonized peoples saw "on their own land, was that people could without punishment seize them, strike them, starve them out. And never was there a teacher of ethics, or a pastor who came to receive the blows in their stead, or to share his bread with them."[11] What the colonized peoples received in material and cultural benefits from the "mother countries" (a characteristic word of colonialist hypocrisy!) cannot be set against this, any more than the self-sacrifice and loyalty of many missionaries to the "natives", though the missionaries stood under the threatening protection of the colonial powers.

This colonial economy is one of the most important sources of our wealth, even today. For by loading these handicaps on the backs of the exploited colonial subject peoples, the western industrial countries have been able to survive the financial losses of two world wars, which they brought upon themselves, and to ensure that even today they can appropriate eighty per cent. of world production for themselves.

This exploitation is not merely an unpaid debt of the past. Political emancipation did not bring economic emancipation to the former colonial lands. Their economy continues to be dependent on foreign capital. Their initial handicap does not let them get their heads above water, and the place of open subjugation and exploitation has been taken by another form of colonialism. During the Geneva Conference on "Church and Society", in 1966, I heard a German delegate boast that he had managed to secure the deletion of the word "neocolonialism" in the report of his section, since it was only a piece of demagogical claptrap. But it was his deletion that was demagogical; the facts are too clear and important for us to be able to question the Third World's right to speak of neocolonialism.

Luckily we lost our colonies as early as 1918. Yet the response among us to that, Hitler's quixotic project of a substitute empire in East Europe for a colonial one, shows that this loss did not mean that we had overcome our inclination for colonial exploitation. The chief matter however is this: that as there is a common European heritage, which marks every one of us, we Germans cannot renounce our share of the common burden of colonial guilt, from which all of us have drawn gigantic profits. Anyone who thinks that we have nothing to do with neocolonialism, should be reminded of our economic—and not merely economic—links with South Africa, and of the expressions of approval by West German politicians who call themselves Christians, on the theme of apartheid.

Now, this is a matter which concerns us not only as Germans, but just as much as white Christians. In his book Winnig draws the "strange picture . . . of the European, thirsty for booty, and dripping with blood, who at the same time feels himself to be the ambassador of the all-merciful universal Redeemer", only at once to draw the sting of this "crying contradiction" by means of the popular irrationalism about a "destiny laid upon us" "that we should by our actions blaspheme against the God whom we confess with sin in our hearts . . . . This is laid upon us, because we are able to bear it."[12] Certainly the victims of colonialism had more to suffer than we had from bearing it, and there can be no word here of "being able." This story of the dealings between the white and the coloured peoples continues to beget accusation and hatred; the message of the gospel is deeply discredited by this crying contradiction, as every Christian in the coloured world is daily reminded. Only forgiveness can open a way into the future. And forgiveness among men can only be procured when the request is accompanied by a sincere will to make reparation.

Here it becomes evident that an individualistic interpretation of repentance cannot grasp what is at stake. Certainly it is the individual in whom the movement of repentance must take place. But the Biblical call to repentance goes forth often not only to individuals, but to whole peoples; it relates to collective guilt, in which the individual is also involved, in cases where he has not himself been a guilty participator, and it challenges the whole collectively to make restitution and to take new ways. The individual, who has enjoyed the fruits of the guilty actions, and has to bear his share of their evil consequences, is challenged to make his effort to bring about a collective change of heart. Our most recent history should prevent us Christians in Germany from losing sight of this connection between the nation and the individual.

2

THE INADEQUACY OF TRADITIONAL CHARITY

The Limits of Charity Hitherto

Charity in the traditional sense, i.e., the alleviation of distress by almsgiving, is not enough, as can be seen from its failure even in the nineteenth century to remove the distress caused by capitalism. Charity is not enough, because such distress is overwhelming. The statistics are known to us, so this requires no justification. "Freedom from Hunger", "Inter-Church Aid", etc., are initiatives about which we are glad, and for which we should be grateful to those who have set them going and continue the work. But they are not more than—let us not use the unfortunate figure of a drop of water on a hot stone, for "What we can do is like a drop of lubricating oil in a piece of hot machinery and not merely like a drop of water hissing uselessly on a stone."[1]

Even a single drop of oil is no more use. "In the year 1965 the contribution of the Church was indeed considerable, but amounted only to one-twentieth of the development aid given by governments, and only one-thirteenth of the investments by private individuals."[2] If the total was, and is, too small, how much more inadequate is our church contribution.

Traditional charity has its picture of the piece of bread that is handed to a hungry man. But there is not only hunger to be appeased, people must be helped to help themselves. Life is always a capacity for individual activity, for self-help. The recipient must not remain the Object of our pity and our benevolent activity, he must himself become Subject. Development aid, which sees the recipients only as Objects, calls forth their shame and fury, and not their gratitude. The leading men of our church aid agencies know this, and would like to give their resources entirely to such projects as serve the native productivity of the developing countries. Cases of acute distress are so frequent and so widespread that this is impossible. Therefore we should look beyond these helpful actions of ours.

Finally, and most important of all, traditional charity is not enough, because it does not aim at the causes of distress, but only cures its symptoms. This is an old tendency of Christian benevolence, which it is essential to overcome today. The reason for this self-limitation is probably twofold:

1. Helper and sufferer are in personal confrontation, the way from the one to the other is short. The sight of the person in need stirs our conscience, and the act of help sets our conscience at rest, because its effect is quickly visible. "Today the commandment of love touches us in such a manner that obedience to it includes a long, tedious way for many groups united in society, many associations, and individuals, a way that we must take together."[3]

2. In the way of help we appear as masters of the situation; we can judge what is necessary, and decide about the means of help we use. But if we start to deal with the causes, then we get into a tangle of problems, which frequently become too complex for us to judge about, and our methods appear ineffective in relation to the causes, and in addition to this, the question about causes undermines our self-confidence, because it might disclose that we ourselves are partly responsible for this condition of distress. So there may be an ideological prudence in not going too boldly into the inquiry about causes.

Karl Barth mentions[4] the striking fact that the movements of renewal in protestant Christianity, from the Reformation down to the Salvation Army, did indeed apply themselves with missionary purpose to the individual, but that they have never felt themselves "summoned to wrestle with the paganism of the old and new *institutions* in the sphere and under the pressure and compulsion of which the life of converted or unconverted Christians, or of men generally, has had to be lived in every age."

They presupposed the *givenness* of the orders and disorders within which individuals had to exist, and held that we simply have to attempt and achieve the best possible in these given circumstances. They left it to "enthusiasts" and notorious non-Christians to attack these orders and disorders, "men who were not interested in Christian faith and its confession, or who misunderstood it, or were even inimical to it", who provided the soil in which these impulses fell and flourished. Religious socialists had then attempted to make clear "the positive significance (the Christian impulses) of certain more or less purely humanitarian a-Christian or even anti-Christian uprisings (such as socialism)," to the Christian Church; but it is still an open question how far this new movement "even in its more modern developments, has really made its way in Christianity. In spite of Evanston and Amsterdam . . . is there not even yet a great and compact Christianity or Christendom which is still asleep in this respect, or at the very best awake and stirred only in the older individualistic lines."

The boundaries of this self-limitation, which has indeed also the character of self-assurance (the assurance that our own judgment is competent, and that our own social basis does not need to be called in question), must today be transcended. In the statements on the problem of development, in the documents of the Church conferences of Geneva, Beirut, and Uppsala, repeated mention is made of structural changes which are necessary, both in the developing countries, and in the developed countries, in order to meet the catastrophes which threaten. To these changes the Church must commit itself. This is one challenge which calls also for alterations of structure and the removal of limitations in theology and in the Church.

God with Us: i.e., with Society

The many points in the wide perspectives thus envisaged cannot here even be enumerated, much less described in detail. If Christian theology has to reflect on Immanuel, God's Covenant with us and for us, the one who is promised to us by the gospel and takes us into his service, then it must ask, what is the meaning of this "Immanuel" for society? What does it mean for mankind in general, which now begins to understand itself as *one* humanity? What does it signify when this Immanuel can be appealed to in the context of technical development, and what does it mean for economics? For example:

1. Righteousness (*Zedakah*) and peace (*Shalom*) are concepts which in the Old Testament are not limited to the individual and his inner life. They have a horizontal as well as a vertical validity, in the relationship to God and in the relationship to the word, and God intends his *Zedakah* and his *Shalom* not only for the individual but for the whole Cosmos. Equally sin, reconciliation, the Kingdom of God and salvation are social realities.

2. The expectation of the Kingdom of God as the total fulfilment of the promise of "Immanuel" does not only have the negative meaning—that it is not we but God alone who can bring about the ultimate consummation, and that every revolution which includes in its programme the realization of the Kingdom of God on earth will come to grief through its own arrogance (and this has hitherto been the sole significance stressed). This expectation means positively—in line with the injunctions of the New Testament—that those who are filled with this expectation have now to bring their lives into conformity with the corporate life of the Kingdom of God, even if it be still under the conditions of this old world. Eschatology and social ethics belong together—this is one of the most important realizations of contemporary theology. From "Behold I make all things new", it follows that new things can and must happen even in our earthly relationships. "It is not from us that the new event originates," said the Metropolitan Ignatius in Uppsala in an important address. "The Church is given, it comes from God." But what use are we making of this gift? That is the real question. As the fellowship with God given to men in Christ, and spread abroad through the agency of the Spirit, the Church is there for the service of *agape*. Everything that does not serve this end comes from the old realm of the letter. "What does not belong to service, belongs to robbery," as Luther has similarly

expressed it. For this reason, at the end of his address, Ignatius spoke of "a cultural revolution" which "demands of us a radical renewal." "Culture in the light of the Parousia, that is the true picture to keep before our eyes."

Faith and Works

The world in which this service of *agape* has to be done, is today a world of hitherto undreamt-of possibilities created by rapid progress, and the same progress has made it a world of unprecedented dangers. It is a world threatened by a catastrophe of hunger on an unexampled scale, where, according to Georg Picht, "more human lives are at stake than were lost in all the wars of world-history".[5] This statement alone indicates clearly that charity in the traditional sense of the word is no longer enough. If God is concerned about our neighbour in distress, as the whole Bible tells us, then that means that God is concerned about the structures and institutions which must be changed to avert the catastrophe of 1980 which has already begun today. Thus God is writing the Order of the Day for the Church, through the agenda of the world, as was said at Uppsala, and so it is important "to preach the gospel in the world's agenda," as was said at the World Conference on Church and Society at Geneva in 1966. It is just this, as we were also reminded there, which gives "the old Church" "a contemporary opportunity to recover one of the essential marks of the Church of Jesus Christ, namely of being a fellowship of service in the world".

This opportunity has brought vividly before our eyes the impossibility today of a theology which tears asunder faith and works by appealing to the true and abiding principle that works do not justify a man in the sight of God. The aim of the gospel is at one and the same time to console our consciences and to mobilize our consoled consciences.

James has his legitimate place in the New Testament, as well as Paul, and only underlines the truth to which Paul himself bears witness. Love is, as Luther said, the self-transcendence, the visible incarnation of faith, without which its inwardness corrupts. "If one turns away his ear from hearing the law, even his prayer is an abomination" (Proverbs 28: 9). But the law sends us forth in the service of love. If sin made the individual a man turned in upon himself, without fellowship, then forgiveness restores the individual again to fellowship. God's forgiving is God's uniting, and God's uniting is God's forgiving, so said Visser t'Hooft in Uppsala, and from there came his saying which has already become famous: "We must be clear about this, that the Church members who in practice deny their responsibility for the needy in any other part of the world, are just as guilty of heresy as those who deny one or other of the Articles of the Faith."

Thus the reformed doctrine of justification does not contradict, but supports those who wish to transcend the traditional limitation of neighbourly love to individual cases. In the Biblical singular "our neighbour" there is concealed a danger to which we must no longer fall victims. This neighbour is not an isolated thing, but, in the words of Marx, a "congeries of social relationships", and anyone who wishes to help him must not limit himself to his needs as an individual, he must alter the social causes as far as that is possible: love today, as Geneva 1966 puts it, must be love in structures. Jan M. Lochman, the Prague theologian, now professor in Basle, was right when he said once recently that a theology of justification, which did not also contain a relationship to society, remained an incomplete Reformation. A theology and preaching which does not continuously reflect upon its social conditioning in order to transcend it, and its social consequences in order to avoid the undesired ones and to promote those which are desired, is an illusionary and egoistic theology, a frustrated Reformation. A "fellowship of service in the world" must share in the world's problems, in the material ones as well as the spiritual ones, if it does not wish to tear asunder body and spirit in an unbiblical manner. Therefore we are today in the middle of an absolutely necessary expansion of Christianity beyond the individual sphere, which is of great positive importance for the discovery of new dimensions of the Biblical gospel. Of this the Catholic theologian Johann Baptist Metz[6] has written, that it is just as important as the demythologizing project (indeed it can be said that it is more important than demythologizing, and can help us to get out of wrong ways of demythologizing!). "The salvation, for which the Christian believer hopes, is not a private salvation. The proclamation of this salvation drove Jesus into a deadly conflict with the public powers of his day. His cross does not stand in the most secret place of the individual and personal realm, nor does it stand in the most holy place of a purely religious realm, it stands beyond the threshold of the guarded private realm, or of the protected purely religious realm; it stands "without" as the theology of the Letter to the Hebrews puts it. The veil of the temple has once and for all been rent in two. The offence and the promise of this salvation are public. This publicity cannot be annulled, dissolved, or hushed up. It accompanies the historical progress of the message of salvation. And in the service of this message the Christian religion has been given a critical and liberating form of public responsibility."

Our young people of today have understood this. That is why they grasp so avidly at sociology. That is why they no longer think existentially, but in marxist terms. That is why the Sozialistischer Deutscher Studentenbund (S.D.S.—the German Socialist Student Federation) have so many recruits among pastors' children, the Student Christian Movement, and past or present theological students. This is not apostasy from Christianity, even if it is sometimes associated with revolt from the Church and with difficulties felt about the Christian Faith. Rather is it the result of what they have heard of the gospel. Parents who are perplexed or even distressed by this, should see in it a proof that one cannot bring up one's children within earshot of the gospel without paying for it. Without our expecting it, they get the idea of testing our social conditions by it, of no longer shutting their eyes to distress even if it be far away in Vietnam and Africa, of striking at the root causes. Thus—*this* is what Bonhoeffer in my opinion meant by his demand for a non-religious interpretation!—to translate religion and Christianity into political terms, to be in quest of love in structures.

3

THE CHALLENGES OF UPPSALA AND THE PROBLEM OF "POLITICAL ACTION IN THE CHURCH"

The List of Challenges

WHAT this means in practice is spelt out for us by the list of tasks which have been set at the Geneva, Beirut, and Uppsala conferences for the churches (and that always means for great church organizations, individual congregations, Christian groups, preachers and individual Christians, all together). The spiritual tasks and external activities of aid mentioned will easily meet with our general approval, and, it is to be hoped, will be put into action. But difficult questions arise in relation to the requirement that the Church must make concrete demands on the State and the populace. Here is a list of such demands, in so far as they apply to the industrial states of the West, taken in the first place from the Report of Section III at Uppsala.

"The churches should:

1. help to ensure that all political parties make development a priority in their programmes;

2. urge and influence the governments of industrialized countries:

(*a*) to undertake international development measures which accord with the expressed interests of the developing countries (e.g. the Charter of Algiers);

(*b*) as a first step, to increase annually the percentage of GNP (Gross National Product) officially transferred as financial resources to developing countries with a minimum of one per cent to be reached by 1971:

(*c*) to conclude agreements stabilizing and supporting at an acceptable level the prices of vulnerable primary products; and providing preferential access to developed markets for the manufactured products of the developing countries;

(*d*) to accept the United Nations recommendations regarding the Second Development Decade;

3. participate in a responsible way in movements for radical structural changes necessary to establish more justice in the society;

4. urge governments to accept, as an alternative to compulsory military service, a term of volunteer service in development work in the volunteer's own country or in another."[1]

Developed nations should:

5. so structure help and trade, that they do not become instruments of the political, ideological and security interests of the developed countries.

Collective international action should aim at:

6. stabilization of the international market (i.e. of the prices of raw materials);

7. a world tax for the creation of a development fund;

8. the diminution of bilateral help by giving support to multilateral help programmes.[2]

The churches encourage:

9. support of the United Nations;

10. signing of the anti-atomic Treaty;

11. multilateral disarmament.[3]

12. removal of military help and private investment from the required one per cent. of State Aid to Development;

13. removal, or at least relaxation of the "conditions of delivery" (i.e. the requirement that monies given in aid should only be spent in the purchase of goods from the donor country);

14. the granting of preferential tariffs, unilateral removal of import barriers, switch-over to industries involving a high degree of technical development in order to aid the simpler industries of the developing countries;

15. measures to ensure that money spent in bilateral aid shall be given under long-term conditions of repayment;

16. measures to ensure easier conditions of debt-repayment;[4]

17. creation of a floating fund for debt-repayment from which money can be drawn without incurring fresh burdens;

18. State encouragement of pressure on private undertakings (and shareholders) to make investments which are in the interest of the receiving countries, and support of such investments and no others (e.g. through guarantees for non-commercial risks);[5]

19. a cessation of the European Common Market's policy of autarky on the agrarian sector. (Klaus Lefringhausen);[6]

20. an increase in the production and reserves of foodstuffs in the developed countries, with a view to the alleviation of acute famine;

21. a re-examination of the priorities in the matters of measures of the cold war and development aid;

22. co-ordination of development aid of the Eastern and Western states, and the development of shared projects;

23. education and posting of advisers, technologists, doctors, nursing sisters, teachers, etc.;

24. a cessation of the brain-drain on qualified specialists from the developing countries;

25. acknowledgement of the final goal; an international sharing of tasks which rests upon the specific contribution of fully-equipped trading with each other on equal terms.[7]

Right and Wrong Intervention of the Church in Politics

This—incomplete—list shows how difficult and extremely complex are the problems of an economic and political nature that the Churches—and that means people who in this respect are mostly amateurs—must now concern themselves. Here they must involve themselves and take sides, make demands and recommendations. This is something strange, not only for charity directed to personal relationships, not only for neighbourly love which thinks in private terms. It seems to contradict flatly the usual division of labour between Church and State based on the traditional doctrine of the Two Kingdoms, and to lead to an "invasion of an alien sphere of responsibility", against which our theological fathers have warned us—and that not only because of the lack of expert knowledge on the part of Church authorities and clergy, but principally because of the danger of confusing the Two Kingdoms, and confusing law and gospel. Here, it is argued, we have to do with matters of reason, and here the Church cannot claim to be wiser than the economic and political experts. If it takes part in a discussion which others understand quite as well as or better than it does, so the thing which it alone can say to man, which is its "real task", and for which alone it can legitimately claim authority, can very easily be lost sight of.

In relation to the tasks "set us by Uppsala", the fears of "the Church's interference in politics" which Bishop Hans-Otto Wölber has expressed, have received much more justification than was given by the memoranda of the Protestant Church in Germany, which gave occasion to them in the first place:[8]

1. The way of the gospel is to change people. Anyone who seeks to change structures takes the way of the law.

2. Anyone who asks the Church to support laudable decisions of the Government, must allow its competence to press for such decisions—and by so doing, gives to the Church the function of a political party.

3. Anyone who regards such tasks as within the Church's competence, must reckon with the fact that

(*a*) he will divide the Church into different parties, because there will always be different opinions about practical questions of this kind, and

(*b*) that possibly some day the Church will be exposed to ridicule when it becomes clear that it has advocated the wrong decisions. To sum up—only in the exceptional case where the Faith is itself at stake, is "the adoption by the general leadership of the Church of a political programme" legitimate; in other cases this should as far as possible be left to unofficial groups and circles. At all costs the specific treasure of the Church is to be guarded: the message of the grace of God, which is offered to all, even to our political opponents.

What is justified in these warnings must be heeded, if we do not wish to commit ourselves to an intervention of the Church in politics like that which necessitated Luther's Reformation and his hard and fast distinction between the tasks of Church and State. Anyone who has been disgusted by the conscious and unconscious political prejudice in favour of the West in protestant Christianity since 1945, expressed in episcopal speeches and Church periodicals—and the unconscious prejudice is the really pernicious and treasonable thing—must realize that the linking up of the Church with another political tendency and the claim of the Church for another political outlook is no less illegitimate. And anyone who has really assimilated the Reformers' understanding of justification, will view with suspicion every legalism in the Church and in its gospel.

Are we then confronted by an Either/Or? Have we no other choice than one between interfering in politics and neutralization of the Church? The way which we have to go has certainly—like every other way on earth—its dangers which we must not lose sight of. But anyone who does not avoid it, either through fear of danger, or because of his own (possibly unconscious) political and ideological prejudices, finds that the nightmare picture conjured up above, dissipates on a closer examination.

1. We must refuse to accept the alternative of having to choose between, on the one hand, the "true" task of the Church, which consists of proclaiming the gospel of Jesus Christ, and on the other hand the perception of political responsibility.[9] The Church has only to do what belongs to its essential task, and nothing that it really has to do is "inessential." Here the distinction is not one between matters of primary and of secondary importance, but at the most a distinction between the centre and the periphery. In the centre stands faith, on the periphery you have works; in the centre the gospel, politics on the periphery; in the centre salvation, on the periphery the well-being of our neighbour.[10]

Between the centre and the periphery our human life revolves, on the periphery is decided and revealed what has happened at the centre. *Fides sola justificat, sed nunquam est sola,* says Luther ("Faith alone justifies, but faith is never alone"). When Faith is genuine, it always finds self-expression in joy and in love. Works in comparison with faith, sanctification in comparison with justification, are not "inessentials", matters of secondary importance, but the articles dealing respectively with justification and with sanctification stand, as the Lutheran fathers said, in relation to each other as *articulus fidei constituens* and *articulus fidei consequens*. The consequences of the gospel are not secondary matters, but its fruit and goal, "created in Christ Jesus for good works" (Eph. 2: 10). Similarly, in my relationship to my fellow-man, my service done for his welfare is not a secondary matter in comparison with my service done for his salvation. The two are inseparable. If his physical misery can bar his way to salvation, his hearing of the gospel, then my service can become a hypocrisy if I concern myself only with his soul and make no sacrifices for his body. "One must be an active man day and night," says Christoph Blumhardt, who simply took it for granted that no hard and fast lines could be drawn between care for a man's salvation and care for his welfare. With his father, Blumhardt profoundly abhored the traditional Christian spirituality which sat so comfortably on the self-satisfied possessors of wealth. He was concerned, day and night, here and there to repel injustice, in defence of man's right to share in God's glory, in order that here and there a man might rejoice in his God-given rights. "If a brother or sister be naked, and destitute of daily food, and one of you say unto them: Depart in peace, be ye warmed and filled; yet notwithstanding ye give them not those things which are needful for the body, what doth it profit?" (James 2: 15 f.) On this passage Adolf Schlatter writes in his commentary; "The word can never fail the believer; with joy he confesses, 'I have faith'. The merciful man gives consolation to the perishing. But here and there, nothing more happens. In both cases, the whole thing is nothing more than a matter of words. Because there is no action, both the faith and the pity lose all value. Such a word is no longer a 'word of truth'."

2. The word "law" must not shock us. Certainly social structures are expressed in laws, but they are not identical with

that law of effort and reward from which the gospel liberates us. Behind such anxieties there stands at this point, in my opinion, the old antithesis of justice and love, regarded as mutually exclusive. But this is not the case. On the contrary, a just state of affairs is one of the ways in which love finds its realization. Justice can be cold and loveless, but love always affirms justice. Love is not indifferent to laws, but seeks to replace unjust laws by just ones. When the Good Samaritan becomes Home Secretary he does not stop doing what he did in the parable, but continues his activity on a new plane, by putting the robbers in handcuffs, and opposing crime by means of social progress. *Maxima caritas lex*, as was said to us at a recent Synod in West Berlin.

3. But what are the relationships between the gospel and reason? Has the Church to preach things that reason is competent to deal with, or does it not, by so doing, remove the content of its message from what God's Word says to us and reason does not, to what we can say to ourselves and for which we do not need any Church? Answer: It is impossible for the interests, competence, and word of the Church to stop at the point where we finish dealing with the revelation that is above all reason, and enter the sphere of human reason. Where faith finds expression in acts of love, it enters into the sphere of reason. What is unreasonable is also loveless. The question is only: What is reasonable? In this matter perhaps the old distinction drawn by our idealist philosophers between reason and understanding can be helpful to us.

Reason is the capacity which sets goals for our action; understanding is the capacity for choosing means fitted to serve our goals. It is clear that in the realm of reason thus defined we can in no case be neutral. There is misdirected reason, which sets bad goals for our actions, as we have experienced in our German history. In the conflict about choice of goals and the highest values, we Christians are already committed: God's love for man in Christ Jesus (Titus 3: 4), makes us lovers of men, makes man the measure of all things for us in political and social action,[11] and thus makes us the allies of all honest humanists, whether they stem from Christian traditions or not.

But after the conflict about goals, there is the conflict of the understanding about the means to the goal, the realm of so-called questions of judgment. Here certainly the Church will be well-advised to choose its words cautiously, because here expert knowledge is essential, and the Christian's power of understanding is certainly no greater than that of non-Christians. But even here there must be no veto on the word of the Church, for,

(*a*) this field cannot be left to specialists, who are apt to lose sight of the end as a critical norm, and unconsciously to let means turn into ends-in-themselves, to let material necessity dictate without being boldly challenged, and to allow considerations of efficiency to override everything else.

(*b*) Many means are not at all morally irrelevant; evil means can destroy good ends, as any student of the history of socialism knows.

(*c*) Anyone who, like the Church, wishes to lead men in a concrete situation to concrete acts of love, must not conscientiously keep his fingers out of the realm of means. Just as God and the devil are interested in details, in the last resort everything depends on the way in which ends are realized. There will indeed be broad sectors in this field which remain the province of the experts, but where their boundary runs cannot be determined *a priori*. Therefore the Church must concern itself with a study of the means and test in a critical spirit the weight of the opposing arguments, inquiring about the interests concealed behind these arguments. Then it will be possible and necessary for the Church in its constituted authority, according to the best of its ability—naturally, how else?—and by its word, to commit itself to one practical answer as opposed to another, as happened in the twenty-five points mentioned above. (See pp. 18–20). Of course it cannot claim revelation as its authority, only rational arguments, and, indeed, in doing so, it may err in detail, and incur ridicule. But self-love should not make it afraid of so doing. The Church's true authority, for which in fact it should feel concern, is not endangered if it is evident that it has not made facile judgments, and that in every case it has been concerned about the connections between the means and the end, and that it can adduce good and important arguments for its decisions. If it avoids this, then it fails in its task of acting as a critical advocate of the end in the realm of means. Then, out of mere devout respect for the expertise of the specialists, it has left unexposed the interests which possibly stand behind their arguments (e.g. the problem of the Atomic Test Ban Treaty cited by Wölber and in the twenty-five points). And then, because it has itself not gone beyond a comfortable verbal approval of ideal goals, it contributes to the result that other people also rest contented with such a verbal approval. As Jürgen Haberma has forcibly put it, "The ideals are so high that they can act as an alibi for serenely disregarding them in practice."[12]

The Church above Party?

The history of the Church is full of such failures caused by self-deception. The challenges of Uppsala place before us the stern alternative of either proclaiming noble ideals which commit us to nothing, in order to assure ourselves of our unity and authority, or of committing ourselves to politics or becoming a group as we have begun to do in the memoranda of the protestant churches in Germany. This certainly does not mean that the Church becomes a political party, and annuls, as Wölber fears "the Christian's non-conformity with the world." The Church has not become political in the bad sense when it thus says yes or no in political questions, but when this yes or no does not follow from a careful listening to the gospel as an attempt to do justice to its contemporary challenge, but is based on other reasons, drawing its inspiration from other sources and other attachments, which will then certainly be "godless attachments." As experience shows, a Church and a piety succumbs to these attachments precisely when it believes that it can be unpolitical—which, in a world where everything is already political, is absolutely impossible. The only refuge from this bad type of meddling with politics is responsible political action, the perception of political responsibility in a carefully tested and critical, above all, self-critical fashion. But this will always involve taking sides. The credibility of the Church does not depend on its neutrality (that is only what people try to persuade us whose interests are painfully touched from time to time by a yes or no from the Church). Its credibility follows from its independence,[13] from the fact that in supporting a party, i.e., taking sides, it does not belong to a party. Only by this will the true "non-conformity of the Christian with the world" become evident from time to time, not by our emphasizing it as an article of faith. Impartiality is a chimera. By venerating it we serve ourselves and not those to whom we are sent.[14]

In my opinion the following principle can be enunciated to guide the Church in legitimate political participation (here I mean the Church's official representatives and organs). The interest guiding such participation must not be that of the Church's self-preservation and the preservation of its privileges, but the interests of peace (i.e., of co-operation and the avoidance of violence and bloodshed), the interests of those who are deprived of secular justice (i.e., equality before the law and a fair share in the products of society), and civil freedom (i.e., the opportunity of responsible self-determination in activity and in helping to share the forms of society). It ought not to take the shape of a permanent alliance with political or social groups, or of membership in a front, but rather of support or opposition in relation to an issue requiring decision in a concrete and particular situation.

Uppsala leaves us no alternative. The gospel leaves us no alternative. "In the budget debates of governments we see very quickly how difficult this is (the application of two per cent. of the yearly gross social product for development aid), because there is no lobby there for the purpose of development itself."[15]

In other cases lobbies represent groups supporting common interests. Here we have to represent the interests of those who have no lobbies in our parliaments. The ecumenical "Conference for World Co-operation in Matters of Development" in Beirut, 21–27 April 1968, which brought together Protestant and Roman Catholic delegates, in its concluding report, challenged the churches and Christians expressly to act as a lobby representing these people; ". . . to subject members of parliaments to a continual barrage of pointed questions, and, if need be, to summon reinforcements" and "... to try to make the result of an election dependent on the attitude of the candidate to development and justice". "The conviction of members of parliaments today (that the citizens are interested in neither) can be shaken if only up to ten or fifteen per cent. of the electorate, who can possibly decide the issue, are stubborn enough."[16] The anxiety that a decision of government would not only be supported by the Church but even extracted from the government under pressure would be an exact reading of the facts. The Church must become a pressure group in questions of development. That this should be claimed as a matter for anxiety is only remarkable because in this moment it is forgotten—a Freudian lapse of memory?—that the Church has always been a pressure group in questions that seemed important to it, from sabbath observance down to religious education. Should it now, all of a sudden, draw back from this role, when the interests of men living far away are at stake? "Open your mouth for the dumb, for the rights of all who are left desolate" (Proverbs 31: 8). So prosaic, so politically dangerous, so "unspiritual" this appears, when one begins to realize it!

4

MORALS AND INTEREST

God's Commandment and Human Interest

ANYONE who comes to men in this world with the challenge of love and justice, must keep the realities in sight, must be "realistic." What is the legitimate place of "realism" in the Christian ethic and proclamation? This question must be carefully considered in order that the commandment, which we have to proclaim to others and to ourselves should not be pared down to fit the existing reality, subjected to it, reduced to its terms, and so bereft of its dynamic by this alteration, nor yet appear as an airy-fairy ideal far above the earth, which by reason of its exalted and remote nature leaves reality untouched. We shall, then, not acknowledge that Max Weber has said the last word with his distinction between an ethic of responsibility and an ethic of disposition; we shall have to overcome this dualism. Two remarks on this point:

1. Christian faith has always acknowledged that God's commandments, taken in earnest, go beyond our natural powers, i.e., contradict our natural will to self-assertion and that a change of heart is necessary if we are to obey them. This conflict has often led Christian ethics to construct a double standard of morality by distinguishing between persons or cases where God's commandment holds good without curtailment, and others in relation to which it must be adapted to reality, and reduced to a compromise. I refer my readers here to the history of the interpretation of the Sermon on the Mount.

Since it is not possible here to discuss this question of compromise in Christian ethics in detail, a reference to our conversations on the question of the atomic, biological, and chemical weapons may suffice. In this question there are two opposing considerations: on the one hand, the knowledge that the unselective mass annihilation for which these so-called weapons are alone designed, even with all the concessions which the Christian ethics of the past have made on the subject of the use of weapons, can no longer be justified in the light of God's commandments, and, on the other hand, the fact that "we are living with the bomb" and therefore are compelled to play politics with it, so long as we have not succeeded in banning the mass weapons. In April 1958 Bishop Lilje said at the Synod of the Protestant Churches in Germany on this subject that anyone who repudiated these weapons must also say to the politicians how they should put this policy into effect in their work. The man who only repudiated them, without taking into consideration all the political consequences, was not speaking responsibly, and therefore was running away from reality. I am today, as I was then, of the opinion that this is wrong, and that it leads to a "realistic" paralyzing of God's commandment, which means that the Church leaves to political calculation the decision of what God has ordained. The consequence of this would be to break the relationship between God's Word and politics, i.e., would be an atheistic policy.

The element of truth in this challenge to share in reflection on the political consequences lies in the fact that it is certainly not enough to acknowledge and give expression to God's commandment as it is revealed to us in the gospel, and then to leave to other people how they are to do justice to it if at all. We are ourselves the people to whom the commandment is directed, we are ourselves in one person both Christians and citizens of the state, and thus politicians. So as Christians, and that means also as the Church which appeals to the politicians, *after* the first step, after hearing, acknowledging, and giving full expression to God's commandment, we must not withdraw from taking the next step, we must consider together with the professional politicians and the experts how to translate this knowledge into practical politics.[1] God's commandment in the question which here concerns us is simple, and without qualifications, "share your bread with the hungry" (Isaiah 58: 7; Ezekiel 18: 16) and "Give to every one who begs from you" (Luke 6: 30). What does this mean in the manifold contexts of responsibility of a government in a highly-developed national economic system? The twenty-five points summarized above are the result of such reflections, intended to foil the repudiation of the divine commandment on the alleged score of its unrealism. Here the aim is to let the commandment make its impact on economic decisions, and thus certainly not to proceed in this matter on the principle "All or nothing". On the contrary, what we have here is an attempt to compromise with the claims of other obligations and the claims of justified self-preservation (all this is contained in the formula "Under the conditions of the old world"), and to put in action at least a limited realization of God's commandment, endeavouring to give it as wide a scope as possible. In doing this we of the Church must not fight shy of political and economic discussion, nor must we leave it to others; we must participate in it.

2. This compromise is the effort to resolve struggle among opposing interests, which must not for that reason be denounced *a priori* as unjustified and sinful. This problem of the conflict of interests is of fundamental significance in social ethics, and this is the cause and the element of truth of the individualistic tendency of traditional Christian ethics: the individual can be challenged and empowered by the Holy Spirit to deny himself and to sacrifice himself wholly for the sake of God and his neighbour.

To challenge a nation to make such a sacrifice is not only unrealistic, but unjustifiable; for a nation consists of many individual neighbours to whom the individual Christians in their midst ought to be just as serviceable as to the men in more distant lands, and a nation does not collectively receive the Holy Spirit who makes one capable of self-sacrifice. It is never legitimate to require a government as the trustee of the people to sacrifice its people for another people or for an ideal. Thus in social ethics the balance of interests plays quite another part from that played in the life of the individual, and compromise here is not an annulment of God's commandment, but that which God commands.

Short-term and Long-term Interests

Thus also in our problem of development aid it is necessary to ask about the interests on our own side as well as the interests which conflict with our effort to give effect to God's commandment to save the starving and create justice in the life of the peoples. Christian realism shows itself, not by watering down God's commandment, but in the realistic analysis of human interests, including those which imperiously demand recognition, and those to which we can make appeal, and those which are opposed to us.

Karl Marx's famous and sobering words, "Ideas always are a laughing-stock if they are not connected to an interest," will be a maxim that we do well to keep in mind. Our whole life consists of conflicting interests, and those people are reckoned clever who can distinguish between short-term and long-term interests, and sacrifice short-term interests to long-term ones. If we acknowledge that it is the duty of a government to protect the interests of its people, then when we call on people to make sacrifices we must be able to indicate how these sacrifices will protect the long-term interests of the people better than their omission. We thus show how far the sacrifices are in the interests of the people itself. Christian social ethics do not require disinterested love from secular collectives, but promise that deeds of mercy are profitable for those who do them and show that in the long run they will profit the collective. It combats short-sighted national egoism, but is in harmony with long-term interests, and thus appeals in political and economic questions not only to love and mercy, but also to prudence, to enlightened self-interest.

Seen as a long-term policy, the prudence of development aid of as intensive a kind as possible, in which we impose upon ourselves *visible* sacrifices, can be easily demonstrated—and that not only as a speculation hoping for a return in gratitude, which is always an exceedingly uncertain factor in the life of the nations. *It is unthinkable that we should enjoy plenty at our well-covered tables, when millions are starving at our side.* Our whole cultural life and our Christianity would not only be discredited by our so doing, but would be inwardly destroyed. "A people that enslaves other peoples," said Abraham Lincoln, "cannot be inwardly free." That is not an idealistic but a realistic statement, which is confirmed by the slaveholding régimes of our time, by the fascist régimes, as by South Africa, and the Stalinistic degeneration of socialism, and recent developments in the United States. That works for a while, but it does not work in the long run and, on those who at first profit by it, takes a bitter revenge, not only inwardly but by the total collapse of cultural life. But externally too we would have to pay a heavy price for adopting this course: China's rise to world-power shows how the hungry will find ways and means of robbing us of the enjoyment of our wealth. "On the day when the hungry masses surge forward, our civilization will go under, and we with it" (Prime Minister Pompidou to the French National Assembly).[2]

It is to the honour of our young people that the thought is intolerable to them that they should be satisfied when others go hungry, and their revolt is a sign that, in such world-conditions, movements of revolutionary solidarity with the hungry will undermine the stability of the affluent society. In his speech at Uppsala, Lord Caradon quoted the following words of U Thant: "There is a prospect that, unless we can limit it, and in the end overcome it, the race conflict will grow to a horror of destruction in comparison with which the religious and ideological conflicts of the past will seem like family quarrels. Such a world will extinguish the possibilities of good in everything that humanity has hitherto achieved, and drag down men to the lowest and most bestial level of intolerance and hatred. For the sake of all of our children, of whatever race and colour, this must not happen." Anyone who is unwilling that our children should become objects of hatred to the coloured world, and victims in the most internecine civil and international wars, must repudiate the fascist way, and take the way of solidarity with the Third World; there is no third alternative.

5

CONSEQUENCES FOR THE LIFE OF THE CHURCH

It is not hard to predict long-term consequences. But prudence is rare, and particularly so in politics, and the resistance of short-term interests is tremendous. Anyone who makes demands acts childishly and idly so long as he does not take into account what obstacles he has to reckon with, what changes are implied by his demands, and what methods he must develop to bring them about. Experience has shown us that in the Church there is an inclination to be satisfied with fine declarations. This is completely false and inconsistent to trusting the Word which befits a Church of the Word. *Ora et labora*, and thus also *praedica et labora* (pray *and* work, and, preach *and* work!) Public life and politics are full of verbal affirmations of high ideals and good resolutions; their function as an alternative to action can be clearly seen by the critics of ideology. We must not play this game, but say only precisely so much as we are resolved to put into practice.

Part of this is that we should first of all make demands on ourselves. In the resolutions of Uppsala, there is among other things quite a list of these, for example, greater efforts at raising money, through gifts and contributions from church funds (the repeatedly mentioned five per cent.), imagination, careful organization and co-ordination of projects in the developing countries (through *Aktion Sühnezeichen* and the different organizations for the service of peace), and so on.

In the last-mentioned matter I would like to point out again how important is the challenge made to our government, and mooted also by the last protestant *Kirchentag* in Hanover,

1967, that service in developing countries should be legally recognized as the equivalent of military service (cf. above, in the Uppsala decision Point 4, on page 19). At the Third World Congress for the Lay Apostolate 1967, the Dutch delegate Thom Kerstiens was greeted by tremendous applause when he said, "Cannot we gradually reach a situation where obligatory military service is replaced by an obligatory social service for men as well as for women? Where men are ready to combat poverty in their own land or abroad, and where girls are ready to give social service to old people, to mentally ill people, and to all sorts of people who have made shipwrecks of their lives? Is it madly Utopian to believe, that if only we would make a beginning, a situation could arise, in which our children, in answer to the question, 'Where did you serve?' would no more answer, 'In the 15th Division' or 'In the Royal Navy', but could answer, 'I served in a hospital in the Congo, or in a school in Cochabamba, or in road-building in Cambodia."[1]

It is no accident that the challenge to do what we must in the field of the Church comes from an ecumenical gathering. It is the fruit of a great thought of the former Archbishop of Uppsala, Nathan Söderblom, who called together the divided Christian Confessions and groups—living side by side as they were in faction and in isolation from each other. He summoned them to share in a service of love in the world, in order that in this way they might find each other, and thus might come to conversation with each other and perhaps to a common affirmation of faith: through Life and Work to Faith and Order. This thought has vindicated itself. This must now happen on the small scale at the grass roots. "The universal Church begins at the local level" is a saying one hears often in the ecumenical movement, a saying too little put into action among us in Germany, less, for example, than in the United States. In the gigantic struggle that is needed against the avalanche of hunger we have God-given opportunity for local ecumenism. As the Consultations in Beirut of Spring, 1968, were shared in equally by the churches affiliated to the World Council, and the Roman Catholic Church, so also the local execution of the task must be accomplished together by all the Christian groups and congregations of the several localities of our country. Then they must seek to draw in other local groups even ones that otherwise are not in sympathy with the Church. Everyone who is willing to co-operate must be welcome in this Oikumene of good will. The encounter occasioned by this work to help the miseries of our time can then lead to a mutual exchange in matters of religious knowledge and melt the rigid exclusiveness of confessional groups.

If we take these tasks seriously, then many customs and organizations of our church life will prove to stand in need of change. Our structures must be first tested to see that they have the new flexibility required by us. I would like to content myself with these few sentences dealing with the subject in so far as it concerns the structures within the Church. Not as though it were of less importance; it is even, as I have said, of the very first importance, and the precondition of all speaking and acting in relation to the outside world. I restrict myself on this subject because, in the other matters, in our turning to the outside world, we are confronted by specially important theological and political difficulties. To these I now return, picking up again the thread of our discussion by dealing with the task of urging our people and our political leaders to take new measures, and with the resistance motivated by short-term interests, which we shall incur when we do so.

6

CRITICISM OF SOCIETY AND CRITICISM OF CAPITALISM AS A TASK OF THE CHURCH

A Lobby for Poor Lazarus

THE fact that such a representative lobby is necessary constitutes one of the greatest difficulties within the larger problem of development. We all know how widespread among our people is the unpopularity of development aid.[1] For this reason if for no other the German National Party, which has based its programme on this feeling of resentment, must not be supported by the votes and contributions of Christians, and we of the churches must say this as emphatically as possible! This point, which deals with the future, is much more important than its retrospective whitewashing of Nazism. Governments and parliaments can claim that this mood among our people justifies their inadequate and harmful development policies. Poor Lazarus is not with us at present, but far away beyond our doors. This is one of the reasons that it is delusive to believe that the Third World can, like Europe, make the grade by its own exertions, as we did in the nineteenth century. Social progress in Europe did not come for moral reasons, though the moral factor among others played a part. Progress was due to the pressures of more material factors:

1. The pressure of the proletariat, organized as a pressure-group,

2. the discovery of the importance of the worker as a consumer,

3. the State's interest in the health of the rising generation for military reasons.

In relation to the first point: the hungry peoples of the Third World are unable to exert pressure on the rich nations either by a kind of trade union organization or by strikes or by the force of arms.

In relation to the second point: in the tremendous development of the home market of the industrial world, these Third World peoples are indeed interesting for the developed nations as producers (especially of raw materials), but not in the same degree as consumers. The profits made by the capitalist economy, especially the American economy, through the armaments race, through limited wars (Vietnam), and through space travel research—undertakings whose costs are borne by the whole world but whose profits are appropriated by individuals—could not be equalled by a changeover of the economic system to development, and consequently to the raising of the level of consumption among the poor peoples. Or at any rate they could not be equalled as a matter of short-term policy. This is the handicap also of all attempts at disarmament in the capitalist world.

In relation to the third point: owing to the over-kill capacity of their armaments, neither of the two blocs of the wealthy world, of course, needs the poor peoples as military allies. They only court them in order to prevent the diminution of their own spheres of influence and, in fact, to extend them as far as possible. The interest which results from this, however, produces a method of development aid which is injurious to the peoples concerned. We shall have to speak of this later.

Thus it seems at first sight quite conceivable that the rich peoples will suffer no material losses, if, as they are already in fact doing, they weaken rather than intensify development aid, and if, while their own table is groaning with food, they calmly let the masses of the Third World starve to death. This is precisely the aim of all those barbarous voices among us that advocate this course, and argue about the necessary decimation of mankind (whose increase has got out of hand) through catastrophes of famine (in which case of course they always mean the starving of other people to death!). The fact that this is barbarous by no means lessens the appeal of this attitude in our barbarous century. Ruling classes in history have always been barbarous when the preservation of their privileges was at stake, and in relation to the Third World we are today the ruling and possessing class.

Thus there is great difficulty in the fact that the population as a whole and the political and economic ruling classes give each other mutual support in their unwillingness to share their goods with the Third World, an unwillingness encouraged by the press, in so far as it is subservient to both parties. Besides this there is the added difficulty that because we have only long-term arguments at our disposal, we seem to have only moral arguments to support us. Morality, however—see Marx!—becomes ridiculous, i.e., reveals its powerlessness, in so far as it is unable to couple itself with material interests. This will be more and more our experience, the more energetically we approach our task.

Structural Changes on Our Part

In the Report of Section III at Uppsala, the first ten years of development were described as a decade of disillusionment, the failure of the Second Conference on World Trade at New Delhi in 1968, the tendency of the industrial states to scale down their development aid, and the tendency towards a new isolationism is mentioned. To counter this, "radical changes of institutions and structures" are demanded, on the three levels of the developing countries, the developed countries, and international economics. "But just because such structural alterations are not set in motion, we see ourselves as a society of nations incapable of doing the good that we would wish to do, and our efforts at international co-operation are thus in danger of being paralyzed."

Let us take one or two examples, from the list of twenty-five points (see pp. 18–20), which will illustrate with particular clarity what trenchant demands on the political and economic system in our country would be implied by them:

Point 19: The agricultural and tariff policies of the European Common Market. In the year of the fruit glut the tendencies to restore protective tariffs *within* the Common Market are revived. Who will help us to reduce the system of tariffs of the Common Market in relation to those outside of it? For innumerable human beings in the southern continents this is a question of life and death.[2]

Points 10–11: For the investments in industry and agriculture required to satisfy the need for food, aid amounting to a capital sum of thirty to forty thousand million dollars annually from the developed countries is necessary. This sum is to be compared with the annual cost of armaments in the whole world, which stands at a hundred and forty thousand million dollars. The relationship is so crazy that everyone will nod in assent when he hears it said that "if we contemplate the repercussion on our future political situation of the failure to solve the problem of hunger, we can easily see that it might be a better protection of our own country to spend the money in rational development aid."[3] But it is one thing to nod one's assent, and quite another thing to act. At the present moment we are not even able to reduce our expenditure on armaments in favour of most urgently necessary investments in educational policy. Will each church present this demand to its Minister of Defence? Will we persuade political parties to support the resolution passed at Uppsala to spend five per cent of our defence budget on development aid?[4]

Armaments and foreign policy are closely connected. Reduction of our armaments is only possible if at the same time stability is being restored to Europe. But stability today is identical with the recognition of the consequences of the Second World War, that is, with the recognition of the present Polish and Czechoslovakian frontiers, and an ending of the German cold civil war that involves the normalization of the relationships between the two German states, by means of a treaty which includes mutual recognition and a solution of the Berlin question. So long as we refuse to acknowledge the *status quo*, and to think ahead from it, we are acting just as blindly as the Arabs in the Near East, we are sacrificing the future for some claim or other to justice arising out of the past (whether a valid or imaginary claim, it does not matter here). To the mountainous problems which are unavoidable we are adding others which could be avoided, and we are spending fantastic sums on the armaments which are thereby made necessary, sums which we urgently need for the overcoming of the problem of hunger. The critics of the memoranda of the Protestant Churches in Germany must therefore be told, "Not only is it impossible to go back on these memoranda, but the task that Uppsala has given us forces us to go beyond the memoranda (concerning Eastern Europe) and peace."[5]

Point 18: Private investments in the developing countries naturally far exceed the assistance granted by states (by about two to one). Are these private investments also to be subsumed under "aid"? What they often are in reality was described at Uppsala in the speech of President K. D. Kaunda as "the new form of imperialism by means of monopoly capital, which in part is the source of endless suffering and injustice." How governments, by measures of insurance against risk, can counter the disinclination of private entrepreneurs to invest in regions of political instability, is mentioned in Point 18. But this only touches a relatively small part of the problem, which President Kaunda described so vividly—and this is nothing less than the problem of capitalism.

Before I begin to deal with this, let us have another look at Points 5 and 8. Today bilateral aid is eleven times as frequent as multilateral. It is understandable why it is so difficult to force governments from bilateral to multilateral. Bilateral aid is useful for the donor country both because of the economic profit which flows back to it, and because of the political profit. It permits the donor to select recipient states according to their attitude to the political interests of the donor country. For West German politics it is a means of hindering the international recognition of the German Democratic Republic. For the politics of the United States (even more involved with military aid than in our case, cf. Point 12), it is a means of imperialistic penetration and domination on a vast scale, of which I shall have to speak in a moment. The international institutions for collecting and distributing the means of multilateral aid exist as yet only in rudimentary form. Not only have they yet to be developed, but for this purpose also there must be worked out a co-ordination and co-operation of Western and Eastern development aid that will go beyond the rudimentary policy of co-existence between the United States and the U.S.S.R. secured by the atomic treaty. This, however, is a wish which, central though its significance may be, today seems Utopian and in any case is naïve so long as it is not accompanied by an exact knowledge of the conflicts which are lacerating the contemporary world. The Third World is both a battlefield and a bone of contention for the East and the West. Its peoples are at once Objects and Subjects in this struggle. Without an analysis of this struggle, the issue of the challenges listed above is nothing but pious self-deception.

Blinkers at Uppsala

At this point one cannot avoid criticising the way in which the churches have handled the development question from Geneva 1966 to Uppsala 1968 and up to the present Synod of the Protestant Churches in Germany. A characteristic of the Uppsala documents is the over-simplified manner in which they speak of the developing countries and the developed countries. This is a generalization which stands in the way of a right understanding. Among the developing countries we must distinguish at least three groups: those whose political independence has the result that the government is at least willing and able to struggle against neo-colonial exploitation; those which are dominated by an alliance between foreign powers and indigenous *compradores* (as is a large part of Latin America); and lastly the four communist states, China, North Korea, North Vietnam, and Cuba. Another tripartite division is possible:[6] those countries in which the production of foodstuffs is growing more quickly than the population (the Western industrial countries, including Australia and New Zealand); those where the two increases are keeping in step (the countries of the Eastern European bloc and the above-mentioned four communist states); and those in which the production of food-stuffs is lagging behind the increase in population. Japan and Mexico belong to the second group, with a tendency towards the first. In the developed countries, however, we cannot loftily ignore the difference between the East and the West in respect of their social structures and economic systems, as Uppsala did.

By ignoring these facts, the documents of Uppsala have failed, in the first place, to indicate to the Christians and churches of the developed countries the specific tasks for them in each developing country. Such undertakings cannot ignore the differences between capitalism and socialism. Contrary to the widespread belief in the East that capitalism and Western imperialism are alone responsible for the catastrophic condition of the Third World, it would have been necessary to show how far socialist governments also fail to measure up (as has once more been demonstrated at the World Trade Conference in New Delhi in 1968), thus showing how socialist governments can succumb to the danger of not acting according to the principles of international socialism, but acting instead from motives of national egoism or pure lust for power.

That the existence of socialist governments is no guarantee of a socialist policy has been shown by the domestic and foreign policy of Stalinism. Today it is enough to refer to the cynical policy of the Soviet government in the Near East, in Nigeria, and in the Czechoslovakian Socialist Republic. The Ecumenical Consultations in Beirut of April 1968 sketched out an appeal to the socialist governments (Chapter I, "The Situation", section 46); citing the need for increase of aid for development, better conditions of trade, priority of aid before political interests, and increased participation in international aid programmes. Had these points been taken up at Uppsala, then the Christians and churches in the communist states would have received suggestions for their situation. This would have been important even although Eastern Christians cannot give expression to such needs in the same manner as the Christians in the Western world, for the self-satisfied view held in the East, that the West is the only guilty party, would then have been corrected. And then we would have had the chance of testing, without prejudice, whether there are advantages in the Eastern development aid which are not purely propaganda but, for example, stem from the fact that no private investments come from the East, and come therefore without any combination of private capitalistic interests and political pressure.[7]

At the same time the element of truth in this opinion would have come to light in a manner at once necessary and disquieting for us. The Eastern bloc contains one sixth of the human race. Even this proportion makes questionable the view with which we flatter ourselves, that the East and the West are equally responsible for the inadequacy in development aid.[8] If we look at all the individual points of complaint, and remove those which concern also the Eastern states, it becomes evident that the most serious complaints are directed against those countries from which, at the same time, greatest contributions to development aid come. Thus, the fact that development aid is largely drained away again through other factors, rendered ineffective, and indeed turned into a kind of development aid *for* the developed countries—into a kind of "blood transfusion in the wrong direction"—is not merely to be laid at the door of the rich countries (as was commonly said at Uppsala) but at the door of the capitalist countries. Anyone who hesitates to take seriously the words "capitalism" and "imperialism" as anything more than the barren claptrap of communist propaganda will only be able to bring forward demands which are "pious platitudes," because they will bear no relationship to the realities which he has failed to discover.

One of the most grievous limitations in the discussions at Uppsala (apart from the lack of time, which explains many inadequacies) was caused by this blinkered attitude. No one ventured to define capitalism and imperialism, although facts were continually being encountered which are covered by these concepts. For all that is contained in the earlier papal social encyclicals, and in *Populorum progressio* (sections 26 and 58), the criticism of capitalism was not taken up. Nor did the criticism of capitalism coming from Protestant circles in the days of religious socialism and most relevant today, fare any better.[9]

The Marxist analysis and critique of capitalism was no more present than at Geneva 1966 and in the German Synods. The representatives of the Eastern churches could not show the relevance of such analysis and critique because, despite their churches' previous outward acceptance of them, they found them still strange. When they make a resolution tending in this direction, it sounds mostly like a mere apologia for the policy of their state and a political attack upon the West. This is connected not only with their relationship to the outer world but with the basic fact that Eastern Marxism is to a large extent today deformed by its scholastic and defensive character. A marxism which is not confined to mere assertions, but is on all sides critical and is developed further to suit the conditions of the contemporary world, would be useful for our orientation at the present day. Indeed it is, in my opinion, indispensable. The Christian-Marxist dialogue, which has come to life again through the participation at long last of Marxists, has to date moved on the plane of philosophical discussion, and therefore has not yet the quality which according to Marxist and Christian standards is to be desired, namely a connection with action and thus with concrete social analyses.[10]

The Absence of the Marxist Voice

The fact that in Church discussions the Marxist voice remains so assiduously excluded, and particularly at a moment in which the young generation is discovering in Marxism an instrument for the articulation of its criticism of society, is equally astonishing and significant. Experts representing various tendencies are brought in, but there is never among them a single one whose criticism approaches the mordancy of the Marxist criticism. It is as if Lord Keynes were one of the Christian Church Fathers, and Karl Marx one of the sinners predestined to reprobation in hell. Here liberal-mindedness and the effort to transcend partiality suddenly finds its limit. A prominent ecumenist in Uppsala justified this to me by saying that after all the Marxists did not stand upon the same ground as we did.

That was honest, but unreflecting. For this means that Christianity and Marxism are once more established as two mutually hostile world-views, a position which we surely wish to leave behind.[11] Disregarding the fact that among the Western Marxists there are some who are free from the anti-religious feeling of the old Marxism and open for a new encounter with the Christian message—especially among the young, Rudi Dutschke being an example—how are the Marxists to be freed from the fatal historical connection of their political economy with atheistic dogma if we on our side, because of this, refuse to take account of their political economy and even to test whether certain things in it might be right, and of importance?

Nothing more than this test is at stake: "test everything; hold fast what is good" (I Thess. 5: 21). If we fail to put things to the test, then we betray the fact that we have already made up our minds and have already taken sides. But is the Church committed to reformism? Does it belong to the Christian creed? If one looks at ecumenical consultations and their leading speakers, it would appear so. By this I do not wish to say anything against these speakers, but everything against the one-sided selection of them. Whether the Marxist critique of capitalism is so irrelevant, so false, so antiquated, as is presupposed in such action, could only be determined when it had been tested in the ecumenical dialogue. If one says these things about the Marxist critique with one's mind made up, and one's eyes calmly closed to those who hold the other view, then that is a sign that this is what we want to think, that indeed we are not free but are determined that this critique should be false.

Further, we have in the German Synods no one who belongs to the group who are the sharpest critics of capitalism, no socialist, no communist, no one to whom the works of the Western critics of capitalism (which every member of the SDS knows), no one to whom the works of Veblen, Baran, Sweezy, Hubermann, and Mandel are so familiar that he could use them in debate. We are all workers, employees, officials or businessmen within our system. The intellectual effort to place oneself, at least in theory, outside our system and to call it in question, ought to come more easily to Christians than to others, since they continually experience the calling in question of their world by the gospel. But instead of this, it is a fact of experience that people outside the Church are freer to transcend the bourgeois system than the churchgoers, with their pastors and synodal decisions.[12] Countless unseen obstructions have got into our heads and take good care that as soon as the capitalist system is called in question and its abandonment is proclaimed as the most urgent requirement of our time, we transform ourselves into apologists of this system, and this at the behest of our theology. Consequently, there is the greatest probability from the start that our synodal consultations and utterances will confine themselves strictly to what can be tolerated within the capitalist system. But this will mean, even more probably, that later Christian generations—perhaps, it is to be hoped, generations in a socialist world—will take note that our synods unfortunately confined themselves within the limits of the existent system, and failed therefore to measure up to the challenge of the gospel in this situation. They will do so with the same embarrassment that we are wont to feel when we note the same failure in many utterances of the Church in past centuries.

For this reason it might be necessary to commission a few people to concern themselves with Marxist view on the problems of development, to bring together Marxists as well as critics of Marxism, and thus to free ourselves from the actual partisanship of the Church in favour of capitalism which, in spite of all protestations to the contrary, has in no way changed among us since the nineteenth century. This partisanship transformed the supposed superiority of the Church to party into a concealment and a means of self-deception.

"*Every People Has Its Nineteenth Century*"

A few indications should make clear the inevitability of such an investigation for a Christian Church that independently and decisively applies itself to the task acknowledged and accepted at Uppsala. We start with the shocking statement which was with us every day at Uppsala: "At the end of the first decade of development, we are forced to observe that the rich are growing richer, and the poor are growing poorer; and that in spite of considerable efforts made on behalf of the entirely new phenomenon in world-history of development aid, and in spite of a not inconsiderable rise of production in the poor countries. The fact that the doctor comes before the agriculturalist into these countries, and that therefore the increase in production at best corresponds to the increase of population, and more commonly lags behind it, is an important reason for this. It is, however, a long way from being the only reason, and does not excuse this development in reverse. It should, in fact, challenge us to even greater efforts."

In this situation we can console ourselves with the statement, "Every people has its nineteenth century." That is, we draw a parallel between the way of evolution that the Third World has to travel, and the way of Europe (more exactly northern and central Europe) since the early days of capitalism. This has the advantage that pessimism gives way to optimism, and the fundamental critique of the capitalist system is reduced to a critique of a few abuses. The task demanded from us by humanity and reason then consists in removing these abuses—especially those that have bad results on the poor countries—in order at least to shorten and ease for the poor countries the painful process of the way from the nineteenth to the twentieth century. At the same time we thus do ourselves the service of protecting our social order from the convulsion which could be inflicted upon it by the starving peoples.[13]

However, those who draw this comforting parallel must therefore overlook the fact that the rise of the Western industrial states who here provide the example for the parallel which is hoped for, in reality has been and is the cause of the underdevelopment of the poor countries. The rise of Western industrialism does not draw the poor countries forward after it as can happen in the relationships within a country, for example in Southern Italy, through the industrialization of North Italy, but hinders them. As we have already said, colonial exploitation was an important cause of this rise to prosperity we mentioned, and the mono-cultures imposed by colonialism. The limitation of colonies to produce raw materials, the methods of private investment and the payment of interest cause this exploitation to continue and are in addition sources of wealth for the developed countries. The depressing result of the first decade of development is thus not a matter of fate, and is not caused by the incapacity of the poor countries to imitate our way, but rather by both the relation of these countries to the capitalistic countries which hinders such imitation and the capitalistic economic system itself.

Neither Pessimism nor Optimism

This does not imply the substitution of a pessimistic dogmatism for an optimistic one. It is not unthinkable that far-reaching reforms in the rich countries which are continually being demanded of them could avoid many of these evils. But anyone who endeavours to achieve these reforms must take a hard look at the interests which stand in the way, and the Marxist analysis is helpful for this purpose.

They are powerful interests. "Tyranny and reaction have a strong and arrogant army, well organized, and very well led," said Lord Caradon at Uppsala. They are interests which do not remain private, but make use of the state for their own purposes. "The State" is an abstract concept which must be given concrete form. Who is going to push through, to translate into reality the measures indicated in our twenty-five points? Officials, ministers, and bureaucracy do not breathe the pure air of noble objectivity, responsible only to their consciences, standing above the troubled conflict of interests. They are exposed to many kinds of pressures. To put it even more strongly, their range of freedom is pretty precisely defined both ideologically and economically. Economic power is political power, however much that fact may be disguised in our form of democracy, and to however large an extent the possessors of economic power may leave the business of politics to professional politicians. In this game, every competitor knows where the shoe pinches, the places at which the big interests are touched. It is in relation to these that it becomes evident where power really lies. Forward looking development aid must be planned on a big scale. Who plans? Who decides about priorities? Who decides about the necessary sacrifices? Who bears the sacrifices? Whose interests are injured, neglected, given preference?

Anyone who has to make challenges of the kind contained in the Uppsala resolutions does well to put these questions frankly to himself, and to inform himself exactly, and then to go with his appeals and his pressures, not only to members of parliament and cabinet ministers, but equally or even primarily to leaders of great industrial concerns like Springer and Henle, General Motors and IBM, Rootes and B.P., and have no illusions about the toughness of the discussion and the list of arguments that he must be prepared to face.

Pessimism is forbidden, scepticism is allowed. The pessimistic view that under capitalist conditions a reasonable policy of development (a long-term policy and therefore in a certain sense an unselfish one) is impossible, is just as wrong as the optimistic view that under socialist conditions such a development policy is automatically guaranteed. Under either kind of system, policy may be more reasonable or unreasonable, more short-sighted and egoistic or more far-sighted and generous. Fascism and the Vietnam war are not the necessary consequences of the capitalist system any more than Stalinism is the necessary result of socialization. Both systems have their tendencies and their dangers, but they consist of human beings who can recognize and avoid these dangers or fall prey to them. In socialism it is not unheard of that the population of a state, precisely when it really controls production and policy, as it should under a socialist régime, should in its trade, tariff, and credit policies treat poorer and smaller countries in a "capitalistic," i.e., egoistic manner. In capitalism it is not unheard of that the tendency to an investment policy of exploitation should be resisted, that a strong government should set its long-range wisdom against the pressures of powerful interests.

Among things that are thinkable, there is a distinction between what is conceivable and what is probable. We must not merely console ourselves with what is thinkable, but we must allow our thinking to be enriched by our experiences, and this means, in all sobriety, scepticism. The historian will not credit the leaders of the German economy with far-seeing policies as characteristic of their tradition, either for the period before 1945 or for that following it. The inner contradictions of the capitalistic system were made tolerable and obscured by favourable conditions and by full employment. But in the problems of development these contradictions are coming to light again. The relationship of demand and profit appeared to the new liberals after 1945 to be excellently balanced through supply and demand on the free market, achieved with the assistance of the state, which secured the equality of handicaps for the competitors. It is a long time since this equilibrium was destroyed. Demand can be manipulated through the suggestion resulting from advertising so that consumption is increased, and supply can be removed from the control of the buyer by means of monopoly. Big business is able to make itself to a large degree independent of the open market, principally because the demand of the state, which has at least as much interest for the profit motive. Its demand, through expenditures on military purposes, space-research, and other projects, makes possible high rates of profit, and also the burdening of the whole populace with the costs of this unfruitful production. The fundamental contradiction of capitalism, the contradiction whereby profits are produced by the work of large numbers of people and appropriated by a few, at the present level of productive powers, creates the interest of the economy in the state as a source of orders and financer of projects whose consumption (necessary for profit) cannot be achieved through the demands of the public but only through exhaustion by limited wars or the need for replacement as technological development creates obsolescence. The demand for development of the infrastructure, the relief of the public from fatiguing work—none of these interests of men in a more human life produce anything like so high a profit, and are therefore reduced to secondary priorities. The first victim in this situation is the solution of the race problem, and the relief of the gigantic poverty in the United States. And if the Third World comes as the bearer of a new demand, then it suffers the same fate. Anyone who complains of the insanity of the profligate expenditure on armaments must make himself acquainted with these associated factors, or at any rate study the analyses relating to this matter.[14]

Furthermore, however, military armament has one further function: in addition to providing an occasion for profit through continual replacement, it retains its original function as an instrument of defence and aggression. This self-contradictory system, capitalism, which steadily fails to produce enough of the materials necessary for life, maintains itself, against attempts to abolish it for its inhumanity and inefficiency. It has been seriously challenged by the conversion of an important group of countries to socialism. But even if the established socialism of the eastern bloc, paralyzed by its bureaucracy, were able to find a means of peaceful co-existence with the capitalistic bloc, by means of which the competition in armaments might be reduced to a tolerable level, this co-existence would be continually endangered both by the rivalry of the systems and the possible impulse to socialism which Western leaders might fear that a better functioning system of the Eastern states might some day give to the Western masses. Further threats to this co-existence, and ones more important today than ever before, would be furnished by the unrest of the Third World, by the new socialist power of China, and by the resulting necessity of the Eastern states to support socialist tendencies in other lands if they do not wish themselves to surrender their character as socialist states.

Peoples on the Way to Socialism

The military armaments of the Western world, especially of its leading power the United States, have the two functions of quick consumption, and the hindering of the expansion of socialism with its diminution of the "free world", that is, the world of the free capitalist interest, together with the protection of capital invested abroad, and the yield of its interest. There are possibly now peoples in the Third World who can no longer console themselves with the above-mentioned parallel with the nineteenth century and with the hope of inner reforms in the capitalist system, peoples for whom the promised development is too long in coming, because in the meantime they are being more and more beggared by capitalism as it is; peoples for whom the wish for national independence and the national exploitation of their natural wealth and their production are becoming powerful incentives. For some of them, through particular circumstances, the middle way of a mixed system with capitalist and socialist elements may be possible (Israel, and perhaps still today Mexico and India?). Others, however, have only the choice either of remaining satellites of America dominated and hindered in their social development by the alliance of foreign oligopolists and indigenous oligarchs, or of attempting the hard, but in their eyes promising, way of socialism (hard, because only central leadership, with a long renunciation of individual freedom, and utilization of the hitherto untapped sources of labour, can make possible the initial accumulation of resources which are the precondition of further economic prosperity).[15]

An Austrian political economist writes on this point: "If the extent and the conditions of development aid remain as they are, and the present prospects for the developing countries are not decisively improved, these countries could be driven to the verge of despair. In this situation the Communist model of development, with its radical destruction of outdated social structures, and the incredible austerities entailed by its compulsory economies, becomes attractive to the intellectuals and the despairing masses. The political presupposition of this way is a more or less terroristic dictatorship. With a few exceptions, the west has failed hitherto to make possible a more humane model of development."[16]

The prospect of these limitations of freedom is naturally

far more repulsive to an observer from the comfortable atmosphere of private freedom and Western prosperity than to a Brazilian day-labourer or a rice-farmer in South Vietnam. The levelling-down to a dreary uniformity is often regarded by the Western observer as the impoverishing consequence of socialization, while the other observer recognizes it as the consequence of the expropriation of the possessing classes, and as the beginning of the end of the misery of the masses. The scale of values and the judgment which results from it depend on the standpoint represented, and it is hard to abstract from this, especially when the information about these countries is so one-sided and confessedly uncomprehending as in the greater part of the western press.[17] But the mishaps, both the unavoidable and the avoidable ones (the mistaken investments, the ideological narrowmindedness and rigidity, "the arrogance of officialdom"), should not prevent us from an interested inquiry as to how these countries have succeeded in overcoming the spectre of hunger.

In the first year of the collection for the fund "Bread for the World", a minister in East Berlin hung up on the door of his manse a placard appealing for the fund with the inscription "Bread for the Hungry in the World". The responsible official of the Socialist East German Party demanded its removal, on the grounds that in the socialist world no one was hungry; he was ready to allow the placard to continue with the text "Bread for the Hungry in the Capitalist World." The man was right; in the communist world hunger has been overcome, whatever the methods may have been. People at Uppsala ought to have been interested in this, if only to discover whether the methods applied to overcome hunger could be purged of their avoidable disadvantages. In the speech by Lady Barbara Ward at Uppsala, the communist countries were only mentioned in a single sentence; examples of successful agricultural development were adduced from India and Japan, but the fact that China, North Korea, North Vietnam, and Cuba had in their own manner climbed out of the gulf between developed and developing countries, was not considered worthy of mention by her or by anyone else. The Conference ought to have greeted with relief the fact that by the removal of the Chinese nation from the hungry masses, their numbers had been reduced by seven hundred millions.

All countries are not equally free to make a change-over to socialism. Only where a revolutionary situation comes into existence as a result of intolerable conditions, can this decision be made in a struggle for power between the revolutionary groups and the holders of power. The question is, whether it is left to the nation concerned, that is, to the victor in this struggle for power, or whether foreign powers do not only support the conflicting groups according to their sympathies, but determine the issue decisively. Guatemala, Santo Domingo, and South Vietnam are the most visible proofs that the United States reserves for itself this right in the case of all countries not yet communist, to determine how far a social change may go, and to hold in readiness and to commit its military forces in order to secure this end. In Latin America the same purpose is served by the maintenance of inflated armies which can only be a threat to their own people, and by the increasing presence of anti-guerrilla instructors from the United States. In Asia the strategy of the "soft war," i.e., the improvement of agricultural conditions under military protection by means of minor reforms with the help of an enormous staff of American protectors, is part of the same policy.

Anyone who makes the demands that the Uppsala list contains, for a reduction of expenditure on armaments, far-reaching replacement of bilateral by multilateral aid, and co-ordination of development projects of the East and West, must be clear about this, that he is demanding a fundamental change in the policies of the developed countries on both sides, and a change, indeed, which should be easier for the governments of the Eastern than for those of the Western bloc, especially the United States, to make. For, in the case of the East European countries, private investments, which the economy requires the State to protect, are not at stake. The more socialism establishes itself, the less the socialist states have to fear a diminution of their share of the world,[18] and as far as its increase is concerned, they ought to be guided by the Marxist insight that revolution cannot be imported, and that socialism only takes root where it is not imposed from without.[19]

Cuba and the United States

The change demanded implies a more radical interference with the policies of the West. Here what is at stake is the surrender of the veto on revolution (which is the present guiding principle of the policy of the United States), in order to leave the decision in the struggle for power in the countries of development to these countries themselves; and the willingness to help even those lands which choose the way to socialism. What is at stake is the decisive giving of priority to the fight against hunger, and the advancement of peace among the peoples, and the soft-pedalling of the interest of powerful economic groups.

Cuba is the most striking example of the opposite tendency in contemporary United States policy. Cuba does not constitute a military threat to the United States, but threatens the interest of the United States monopoly in Latin America through the danger of infection of the Latin American peoples from the Cuban Revolution. The fiasco of the affair of the Bay of Pigs (April 1961) has not prevented the leading groups in the United States from subjecting Cuba for the last eight years to a murderous hunger-blockade, in which they have compelled most of the Latin American states, and, as far as possible, the trade and the governments of the NATO states, to participate. The intention of this blockade is murderous. If it has not led to the hoped-for capitulation of Cuba, and the restoration of capitalism there and the exploitation by United States capital. This is due only to the natural wealth of the island, the support of Fidel Castro by the people, and the help of the Eastern bloc. The intention was that in the heart of the struggle beginning against world hunger, a people which by great effort had raised itself above its previous misery, should be thrust into misery again, and made tractable through hunger. The World Council of Churches at Uppsala was, with its admittedly very moderately expressed statement, the occasion of the first protest on the part of the Church against this scandalous policy. "The lifting of the economic blockade of Cuba would be an example of the kind of change in attitude we are describing" (namely of using the policy of development as "the instruments of their own political, ideological and security interests").[20]

Only at this point do the Uppsala documents explicitly specify what they elsewhere leave veiled in general undifferentiated terms and demands. Anyone who speaks today of world hunger and development policy must speak critically of all sides, of socialism and capitalism, and of that country which today possesses the greatest military and economic power—a power unprecedented in human history, held by a country whose decisions thus mean calamity or progress for all countries—the United States. Otherwise everything remains in darkness and illusion; moral demands are made that have no motive power because they commit themselves to nothing concrete. "The day when the United States is converted on the issue of the economic and social situation of the world," says Helder Camara, the Archbishop of Recife, "the day when the United States decides to make a thoroughgoing investigation of the politics of international trade, and to require all the other countries to make such an investigation—because this is the only way in which a harmonious and integrated progress can be achieved, that day will bring the world nearer to peace than the elimination of all the stocks of nuclear weapons in the world."[21] The word "conversion" is used here, not only because it is part of a priest's vocabulary, but because what is necessary is in actual fact a conversion, a profound change of heart, the renunciation of an old tradition of rivalry, competitive and acquisitive thinking, so that the United States may no longer stand in the way of world development and drive it into disastrous blind alleys. The churches in the United States are beginning to perceive their responsibility and to work for a collective change of heart,[22] while we are still entangled in the academic theological discussion as to whether only individuals, or a collective also can be converted. By asking this question we are shutting our eyes to reciprocal influences which urgently demand attention in the context of the theme which is before us.

I do not mention the United States either out of anti-American bias, or because a scapegoat is felt to be necessary. Both these motives would be as crazy as they are un-Christian. The United States must be mentioned simply because of its greatness and because of the facts. But in addition to this, when I speak of the United States, I do not leave Germany out of account. Militarily and economically West Germany has closer links with the United States than has any other European country. As Averell Harriman acknowledged, the Germans have given more help to the American intervention in Vietnam, and showed a greater understanding of it than all the other European countries. Changes of heart and policy in the United States would involve just the same changes in Germany, otherwise it might be that failure to make them here would lead to a similar failure to change on the other side of the Atlantic.

7

REVOLUTION AS THE THEME OF CHRISTIAN SOCIAL ETHICS

THE veto of the Church's tradition on revolution corresponds to the veto of United States politics on revolution. The fact that since the Geneva Conference of 1966 at least, the watchword "revolution" is echoing through the Church, is regarded by some as a mere passing fashion. Already there are theologians who are using the first attempts to face up to the problem of revolution, in order to construct an abstract idealistic system of a Theology of Revolution, which is then to be demolished by academic criticism[1] in order that the disquiet which is awakened by these attempts be not too disturbing. The first aim of these attempts[2] is to break down the anti-revolutionary dogma which has dominated the Church since Constantine and has made it, in spite of all its claims to be above party, the ally of conservatism and the counter-revolution. This dogmatic veto on revolution confronted the European proletariat in the nineteenth century with the choice between revolution and the religion which forbade it, and the proletariat then opted for revolution, though admittedly it later renounced it. Today the question is whether revolutionary movements in other lands must once more be confronted with this choice,[3] or whether an understanding of the Christian message is possible which permits—with whatever provisos may be added, the possibility of deciding for revolution.

At Uppsala, after M. M. Thomas's magnificent address on "Questions concerning the Life and Work of the Church in a Revolutionary World",[4] a delegate passionately warned the

Council that by modifying its veto on revolution the Church would incur a share of the responsibility for the "destruction of the world," and some other criticism expressed after this address was in the same vein. But this sort of thing will no longer do in the century of revolutions. As a part of the criticism of ideologies, we shall have to point out that it is possible that this veto is inspired by the prejudice resulting from membership in the class and order of society threatened by the revolution, so that necessary self-criticism may precede all further reflections. The first thing that a man who utters such an uncompromising veto must be asked to explain, is how he would prevent the exploitation of his veto to reinforce the powers interested in consolidating the *status quo* and their counter-revolution.

The Problem of Force

Then the discussion usually gets bogged down in the problem of *force*, and it is indeed the use of force by revolutionaries which is so shocking to our tradition. This too will be a tasty morsel for the critic of ideologies. For the same churches which have vetoed revolution on the grounds of its use of force, have by no means always universally preached unconditional renunciation of force, but have always approved of its use, though admittedly under very definite conditions and to a very limited degree, that is, when it was used by the authority that was in possession of the legal monopoly of force, the *legitima potestas*, the "authorities". From this standpoint, these churches have developed a doctrine not only of the legitimate use of force by the police, but also of the "just war", which it is easy today in the age of unbridled war to laugh at, and to condemn but which in its day was a serious attempt to restrain the demonic use of force. If in this way the possibility of the legitimate use of force and the legitimate participation of Christians in the use of it are conceded, then it is not possible all at once to start a polemic against the revolutionary use of force in the name of the renunciation of force. Anyone who believes military service to be compatible with Christian existence and participation in a revolution achieved by force not thus compatible, anyone who is not a pacifist in his attitude to war but a pacifist in relation to revolution, does not balance his books. For, exactly the same conditions, under which Christian ethics has hitherto affirmed the use of force by the state as *ultima ratio*, and the same exhortations, with which it has accompanied this permission, hold good also in the case of revolutionary force.[5] Anyone who makes a special case against the latter, as is common today among people of moderate views, betrays that for him war and military force are a smaller problem than revolution.

But is revolution really more problematic for a Christianity that takes itself in earnest? All use of force must indeed be profoundly problematic for us, much more than for the Christians of past centuries. Anyone who listens to the gospel cannot find force, and especially the act of killing, anything but horrible. The situations in which in spite of this horror he can overcome this reluctance and share in the use of force must be exceptional. It is singular enough that in the same days in which we are becoming more aware of this than our fathers, because of the growing bestiality of war, days in which Christian pacifism must be our normal attitude, the problem of force is posed for us from the other side, no longer in relation to the place and task of the government in defending the given system of law, but in relation to the effort to overthrow this ordered system. And it is a problem that we must think through.[6]

It becomes urgent in those situations in which we are faced by a government system which creates and perpetuates injustice and misery. Revolutions that seriously pose the question of the justification of the use of force are thus those and those only where there is need to remove intolerable conditions, to secure better laws and conditions worthier of human beings, that is, not fascist but democratic and socialist revolutions. The *problem* arises here as to whether this question can be answered in the affirmative. Here only general criteria for testing can be given. The decision must be made in each concrete case.

Anyone who denies the possibility of a *revolutio justa* and at the same time supports military force because of the possibility of a *bellum justum*, cannot do so in the name of non-violence, but only on the ground of a claim that the *legitima potestas*, the existing legal authority, is inviolable. But what Christian justification could really be given for this claim, unless appeal were made in the traditional manner to Romans 13, taken in isolation and regarded unhistorically, as if the relation of the Christian to political life and to the use of force could be exhaustively described in terms of this text and this text alone. The words which M. M. Thomas quoted from *Frontier* (Spring 1968, p. 51) seem to me incontestable: "From now onwards the just revolution must be treated as on a par with the just war. This will be disagreeable both for conservatives and for progressives. Anyone who regards revolution by force as a suitable weapon for political change, will be inclined to condemn war as an instrument of national policy, and vice versa. Let us consider the matter objectively. If there are few just wars, there are probably just as few just revolutions, with their built-in danger of civil war. But if there are any just wars, then there are also some just revolutions."

But if force *is* to be used, then it can sooner be justified where it is applied to shattering unjust oppressive force than to maintaining it. It is better that the decision to use force should stem from pity for the disenfranchisement and humiliation of men, rather than from obedience to the commands of the powers that be. If force *is* to be used, with great reluctance, then the *revolutio justa* must be less uncongenial to Christians than the *bellum justum*.

In the Report of Section IV at Uppsala ("Towards Justice and Peace in International Affairs") there is a detailed treatment of the subject of conventional and atomic wars. The word "revolution" is avoided; in Section III on the question of "Economic Justice" it is then stated that: "Some Christians will be among those who, despairing of the removal or reduction of economic injustice by peaceful means, feel obliged to have recourse to violence as a last resort. In such circumstances, both violent action and passive inaction come under God's judgment. Since recourse to violence could end in a defeat for both justice and order, special attention should be paid to non-violent strategies for the achievement of change."[7]

Because of the Christian aversion to violence we must at once agree with the last sentence. But the whole paragraph, with its subsumption under the economic question, as if this were the only question at stake, and with its formulation (in the first draft the first sentence began with the words "Some Christians will be among those who . . ."), shows that here the participation of Christians in a revolution is regarded as exceptional, only as "an extreme instance of Christian engagement,"[8] as a desperate and exceptionally questionable decision—as a similar case to "absolute pacifism" which is mentioned in the first section as the standpoint of "some Christians." Thus, here, armed service in the regular forces is regarded as the normal thing for Christians, and is obviously judged as much less questionable. These armies, equipped with conventional and atomic weapons, are recruited for the most part from baptized Christians and Church members. They are sworn to obedience by taking an oath, most frequently in religious form, and the great churches support the taking of these oaths with their moral authority. The oath is the moral cement which is added to military discipline and its methods of compulsion. Thanks to this whole structure of external and internal compulsion, great masses of men are placed willy-nilly at the disposal of the actual holders of power, for the crushing of the oppressed (Latin America), for colonial wars (France in Algiers, the United States in Vietnam), for the strangulation of other peoples (Soviet troops in the German Democratic Republic on 17 June 1953, in Hungary in 1956, and in Czechoslovakia in 1968), for overthrowing a democracy by a *coup d'etat* (Greece). This is how the great and small bureaucrats, Hitler and many others, are able to realize their unholy plans. Which is more questionable, which is an "extreme Christian engagement"; the dropping of anti-personnel bombs and napalm on Vietnamese villages by United States pilots, who in the trials after their capture nearly all affirm themselves to be loyal Christians and Church members,[9] the shooting down of a demonstrating mob in obedience to orders, or the participation in guerrilla activities in order to overthrow the oppressor? Why does the Uppsala Report never even mention the fact that the first people to resort to force are not the revolutionaries, but that the force they use is used subsequent to, and in opposition to, the preceding force of the oppressors? Should then the sequence not run as follows:

1. The normal and most obvious policy for the Christian is absolute pacifism.

2. In responsible love for suffering mankind he will, in certain situations, resolve to participate in forcible revolution.

3. It can only be "an extreme of Christian engagement", if in mere obedience, without making a judgment of his own, he executes commands to kill.

4. This extreme is further impossible, where the immorality of individual commands or of the war in question is recognized.

Christian reactions to revolution in a revolutionary time will be erroneous so long as people concentrate on the problem of force, isolate it, and in so doing forget everything that they have said in the context of the police, the army and war, about the possible inevitability of force in the service of justice and love. The essence of a genuine revolution is the overthrow of the power structure. "A radical change in the power structure as the means to social justice, this and not violent action is the essence of revolution . . . . Therefore we can . . . say, that force is the *bene esse*, but not the *esse* of revolution." (That is, it may bring about the success of revolution, but is not an essential ingredient of it.) Thus M. M. Thomas put it pertinently and emphatically in his address, adopting a terminology customary in the ecumenical movement, which is used in answering the question whether a church tradition belongs to the "being" or merely to the "well-being" of the Church; that is, whether it is indispensable or not. The phenomenon of revolution has many aspects, and we took up this problem only to refute the objections which this problem of force is apt to create. I know of no better way of closing this section than by quoting words of Helder Camara, in an address on the question, "Is force the only way out?"[10]

"Allow me to put it in simple, straightforward terms. I honour those who feel themselves compelled by conscience to opt for the use of force—not the all too easy force of the *salon-*

guerilleros, but the use of force by those who have proved their sincerity by the sacrifice of their lives. It seems to me that the memory of Camillo Torres and Che Guevara deserve just as much respect as the name of the Reverend Martin Luther King. The man whom I accuse, is the real user of violence; all who, on the right or the left, outrage justice and stand in the way of peace; I myself believe that I must take the way of a pilgrim for peace; personally I would a thousand times rather be murdered, than kill others myself."

8

DEMOCRATIZATION AS A CONSEQUENCE OF THE NEW POLICY OF DEVELOPMENT

"Responsible Society"—Interpreted at Uppsala

TRADITIONAL charity is not enough. In these pages the word "aid" has often been used—as an abbreviation, so to speak—but it is misleading. "Development aid" by the "developed countries"—this sounds as if it were a case of helping a poorer climber up to the top of the mountain on which we ourselves stand. Our own status is then made a norm by which others are measured, as if there could be no greater good fortune for them than to arrive at the stage that we have reached. But this is still thinking in colonialist terms. The call for structural changes is not merely one that is directed from the developed countries to the developing countries with reference to their outmoded traditions and institutions, in so far as these are obstructing modes of production necessary to master the new situation. This situation demands also in the developed countries "radical changes in institutions and structures" (Report of Section III), a "change in structure as a moral achievement."[1] In which direction should this change move?

Uppsala answered this question with indications that safeguard the concept of a "responsible society" current in the ecumenical movement from being confused with a merely formal democracy, a misunderstanding which had sometimes threatened. These indications show that what is intended is a dynamic remoulding of the whole life of society along democratic lines. In the Report of Section IV we read, "Churches should strive to make their congregations feel that in the modern world-wide community the rights of the individual are inevitably bound up with the struggle for a better standard of living for the underprivileged of all nations" (Report, p. 64), and "respect for human dignity, equality and the free expression of thought even in print" and "the active engagement of people of all ages in development, reconciliation and social work" are mentioned in this context, as are the rights of minorities, and the removal of all racial discrimination, all this with the purpose of "realization of social justice in all human relationships".

The Report of Section VI ("Towards New Styles of Living") speaks in the same tenor when it says that "In our time many efforts of renewal are identifiable by their commitment to the struggle for social justice" (p. 93), and further, "Where there is a living protest against selfish accumulation of wealth, where a foreigner is respected as a colleague and welcomed as a neighbour, in those who stand up for the rights of minorities —there we find ambassadors of reconciliation in our time" (p. 91). It welcomes therefore the revolt of the young against rigid authoritarianism and institutions which resist the challenges of the "new world", and mentions as a task of Christian encounter with power the breaking of the chains of violence which begets violence, in order to foster the freedom of men to live together in mutual respect.

In the Report of this Section, one description among others given of the Church is a community of people "who have a hope and a message for the world, who are capable of forgiving, who fight for economic justice and human dignity, who are concerned for the sick and the despised, who support and defend the responsible freedom of scientific research and the arts" (p. 88). In the same vein the Report of Section I ("The Holy Spirit and the Catholicity of the Church") says, "No church can properly avoid responsibility for the life of its own nation and culture" (p. 17). One of the denials of the Catholicity of the Church is seen in the belief of Christian communities that they can "allow their membership to be determined by discrimination based on race, wealth, social class, or education" (p. 14).

One of the "new implications" which we discover when we engage with this world "as the place where God is already at work to make all things new and where he summons us to work with him" (p. 12) is the implication resulting from the unity of all mankind in Christ. "Renewal must begin in the local community, by detecting and dethroning all exclusiveness of race and class and by fighting all economic, political and social degradation and exploitation of men" (p. 18).

The message of the Council concluded by making a direct connection between its motto, "Behold I make all things new" (Rev. 21: 5), and the "cry of those who long for peace", the hungry, the exploited, the condemned and the underprivileged. The eschatological hope is regarded not as a consoling sedative, but as a summons to action: "We ask you, trusting in God's renewing power, to join in these anticipations of God's Kingdom, showing now something of the newness which Christ will complete" (p. 5).

These are great and urgent words. But where do they point? Clearly what they imply is something more than an effort in aid of distant and hungry nations. They compel us to ask the question whether all that is still needed is social justice merely in other continents, and not also at home. They do not permit us to make this concession in a merely general undertone of resignation about this world on the grounds that of course nothing on earth is perfect, and that some things in our society still need to be improved. The enormous productivity of our economy, our twenty years of immunity from wars within Europe, and the new methods of dealing with crises, have created a prosperity in which all classes of the population share, and which has preserved for us the democratic freedoms restored to us by the overthrow of the Hitler state, without their having been endangered by economic crises. So we are living in an idyll in the midst of the enormous tensions which are tearing the world apart. For this reason all critical questioning of our situation is customarily countered by the defence that it contrasts favourably with conditions under the brown dictatorship and the red. There is little inclination to think beyond our present order of society. Even the undeniable involvement of our life here with the rest of the world impels few to ask whether these tensions are not operating silently among us also, and may not one day become so manifest that our contentment may come to a bitter end; whether we are not drawing dividends from the poverty of other countries; and whether we are not already heading for the loss of our present freedoms, a loss which we shall only realize when it is too late. Through its degeneration under Stalin, through economic mistakes, and through the lack of opportunities for the consumer in the countries of Eastern Europe, socialism has been so discredited that it does not appear worthy of consideration as a possible alternative to our present system. So we cut our coat according to our cloth, and are satisfied that for the time being we have it so good.

Democratization—Goal of the Student Revolt

The revolt of the young[2] has startled people out of this mixture of resignation and grateful contentment; that is why people are so angry with them. People try in many ways to neutralize the revolt, concentrate on unpleasant and untypical marginal phenomena and play them up. In order that they may spare themselves a careful examination of the thing that is being said, they get indignant with the methods of saying it. People explain things in psychological terms: youth's need for opposition and sensationalism; the satiety of affluent bourgeois young people, which will lessen with the coming of maturity; or the idealistic perfectionism which will not be satisfied with the imperfections of even the most successful democracy. People betray by this that they are not glad of things which ought to make them rejoice, if they took the liberal faith seriously:

that the young generation is becoming interested in politics, and no longer favours individualistic aestheticism and esoteric existentialism;

that it keeps watch with a vigilant and jealous eye over the democratic freedoms;

that its thought is not bounded by national frontiers, and that it has anticipated the older generation in breaking through the sterile East-West confrontation, and sees in the development of the Third World a condition of its own future;

that it cannot endure to enjoy prosperity when others are starving;

that it has opted out of "keeping up with the Jones's" and cannot regard the meaning of life as exhausted by a further rise in living standards and promising careers;

that it loathes the fascist superman thinking;

that it can only breathe the air of freedom, and has realized that freedom is either everyone's freedom or nobody's freedom.

These are the motives for this generation's revolt, and in this it is exactly in line with the tendency of the statements of Uppsala we have quoted. But because it is not yet corroded by resignation (and that is only the "right of youth" about which older people are accustomed to smile wearily, though that is youth's function of renewal in the corporate life of the generations), it takes in earnest what is only verbally proclaimed in its hearing. It asks what is the binding force of the great words of freedom, justice, human dignity, and self-determination, which also recur constantly in the Uppsala documents. It does not leave them hanging in the heaven of ideals, but takes them as norms for its concrete critique of society, and as an instrument of this critique, the Marxist analysis, which its middle-class fathers ignored, shunned, and buried with premature and prejudiced haste. And with this analysis it accepts the accompanying promise of an alternative, the alternative of a socialist society which we do not yet know, but of which in the States that call themselves socialist there exist certain foreshadowings, a society which stands before us only in Utopian outlines and as an object of hope.

If here we have only the idealism of young people, of which we can expect that it will shipwreck on the reefs of reality, then we might wait until the excitement dies down, and gives way to another craze. Then it might be that the statements of Uppsala come under the same judgment, for we have seen how strikingly the efforts of the young people correspond with them. If both point in the same direction, then that is an indication to the Church that it should ally itself with this movement of the young people. The fact that they refuse to accept the world as it is should not appear strange to us in the light of the gospel, which so clearly summons men from a way of life dictated by the old world into one determined by the expectation of the new world of God and the vision of a new communal life of men in freedom and brotherhood. It was a heresy which we had long ago recognized as such (see Uppsala!) that the Christian message of the Kingdom of God was only a sedative, a comforting heavenly consolation in the misery of the irredeemable world, and not—in addition to the consolation that it truly gives for what is irredeemable in this world—at the same time a motive to change, and indeed to change into greater conformity with this vision what can be changed. If the bourgeois society as we have it appears relatively acceptable to some because of the advantages they enjoy from it, and to others unacceptable because of the injustices, limitations and frustrations immanent in it, then is it surprising that so many Christians and churchmen are more likely to be found among the former, when one would expect them, if one hears the Bible as a living voice, among the latter? So far as this is the case, it only the more forcefully confirms the Marxist critique of religion, which, less interested in religious ideals than in the actual behaviour of religious bodies, regards this behaviour as a reflection of the society in question, thus asserting the inevitable domination of religion by social interests. This theory can only be disproved by action. This is happening today in many places through the action of individuals and Christian groups, and is beginning to have its effect on Marxist prejudice. "*Savez-vous qu'il existait encore des chretiens?*" (Did you know that Christians still existed?) This was written by Paris students on the wall of the Sorbonne.

The motive that inspires the young people is by no means a mere exaggerated idealism, but a very clear recognition of the dangers that we have to face today and the decisions that have to be taken, by which their future will be determined. It is significant that an important impulse to the young people in their opposition in the West German Republic was given by the recommendations of the Scientific Commission on University Reform (1966).[3] These provided striking proof for them of the indissoluble connection between university reform and the changing of society, and the dependence of the ideas on university reform upon the contemporary understanding of society. The proposals of the Scientific Commission—on which, in addition to university teachers, the chief interest represented was big business—were controlled by "How can our school and university-system work more effectively to satisfy the demand of business and management for qualified specialists?" The human beings for whom participation in intellectual activity should be a way of self-realization, and who through this participation should be equipped as members of society, persons of independent judgment sharing in responsibility for society, were regarded as of comparatively slight importance. The encounter with science here would not lead to emancipation, to the attainment of maturity, but would train people for the performance of limited functions. This document of the Scientific Commission was for the students—and to their shame be it said, not to anything like the same extent for their professors—a signal pointing in the direction of a technocratically organized and consequently servile society, and was therefore a signal that alarmed them. By this they realized that the greatest danger that threatens democracy is not that of totalitarian tyrants, who however atrocious they may be, prove again and again to be conquerable. The greatest danger comes from a totalitarian technocracy which surreptitiously comes to power, and is so particularly hard to restrain because it is the product of technological progress itself. (For this point the analyses of Herbert Marcuse are instructive.) And yet this technocracy is at the same time unable to lead us out of the contradictions of the capitalist system and its consequences, which are most clearly visible in the Third World. (This is where Marcuse has his limits, but is the point at which the analyses of the newer Marxist writers begin.)

Technocracy or Democracy

What the Uppsala documents desiderate is a struggle for justice, human dignity, and self-determination, and that means today nothing less than *democratization.* This is the paradox of our situation: at the same time in which the knowledge of the identity of democracy and a humane society has so established itself that even in Christian ethics an ecumenical consensus on this point has been reached, in this very same time the possibility of democracy is in such peril that in spite of all lip-service paid to it, countless people (and not only in the lower classes of the populace, who have always had daily painful experience of the limits of middle-class democracy, but also many intellectuals and politicians) are already resigning themselves to the impossibility of democracy. Every technical advance increases the inter-dependence of society, lessens the independence of the individual, increases with man's dominion over nature also the possibility of man's dominion over man. The same technical progress drives to ever-greater concentration of capital, to the creation of trusts and cartel agreements, which reach far beyond national frontiers; the free employer and free competition sink to the status of legend from the good old, so recently past, times of neo-liberalism, but still are useful as a propagandist defence against socialist collectivism. The capitalism of the great monopolists is at best a rationalized absolutism of gods who are emancipated from all control from below, and whose decisions none of those whom they dominate can question. The only norm is material necessity, to which they appeal in order to justify themselves in the face of all humane demands; and what Helmut Schelsky writes of their tools, the politicians, is true also of them. "For the 'statesman of the technical State' this (norm) is neither the expression of the will of the people, nor the embodiment of the nation, neither the creation of God nor the vehicle of a missionary idea, neither an instrument of humanity, nor that of a class. The material compulsion of technical means which demand to be served under the principle of a maximum capacity of function or achievement, removes all necessity of asking these philosophical questions about the nature of the State." What here appear to be able to "demand" are apparently only the technical means, while the question of the end and purpose of their maximal function obviously belongs to discarded metaphysics. Or is this purpose the satisfaction of mens' needs? But those who are thus dominated (and their numbers have been inflated beyond measure) are themselves now only the means, whether as a source of labour, or as consumers of the products created by this apparatus, which appears to be an end in itself. "The dependence characteristic of the industrial form of business spreads through the whole social system . . . . Through interdependence industrial society becomes in ever-increasing measure a unitary industrial structure, which can only function as a unity, if its component industries function co-operatively. Disturbances in parts of the structure lead to disturbances in the general industrial structure of society" (Eric Voegelin). The only movement in this monster structure below the level of the supreme gods is that of subordinate functionaries, to which category belong even those produced by the universities. "Their situation is conditioned precisely by their specialization, and their dependence on superiors, and further by the business organization, which even in the realm of science takes on an increasingly bureaucratic and industrial character. This new army of scientific employees has a constantly diminishing share in the glittering prestige and the relative freedom of the old type of scientist"[4] (Hans Paul Bahrdt).

Admittedly this apparently self-sufficient system rotating on its own axis is not so devoid of all human quality as its theoreticians paint it. This human (though admittedly not humane) element is the interest of the supreme gods and all those whom they have secured as their junior partners in the rate of profit, in the exercise of power over men, and in the maintenance of a residual element of competition which will still be present[5] when in a few years' time the whole Western economy is dominated by three hundred giant concerns, as political economists prophesy it will be.[6]

If this is what we are coming to, then the history of mankind has not been, as Hegel dreamt, a way to freedom, but to perfect, though admittedly well-fed slavery; a process in which automation does not lead to freedom, but only to leisure with its *panis et circenses* (bread and circuses); a system in which "the worker is as little the master of his fate as the ants are masters of the ant-heap" (De Gaulle during the May disturbances of 1968). It is a far cry from this society to the "responsible society" of the ecumenicals, to exhortations to exercise Christian freedom in love; these can now be meaningful only in private relationships, because in other matters material necessity and instructions from above have taken over, and because responsibility which goes beyond the private sphere and the limits of its partial function has been transferred to those high gods who alone are now permitted to be responsible persons.

It is astonishing that H.-O. Wölber[7] quotes so calmly von Weizsäcker's conjecture that the age of coming world peace could "possibly be the most dreadful slavery" without noticing what is theologically at stake. On the contrary, following a bad tradition of Lutheranism, he sees in this only a confirmation that the world after all is evil, and then he continues: "Material necessities are thus not errors of construction which we might be able to change. We must reflect on the fact that they are the expression of a world "that lieth in wickedness". What then can be made of the "freedom of the person" of which he speaks next? How far it can then be anything more than a self-enclosed subjectivity which for anyone else is of no interest, since it has no possibility of freedom towards the outside world, no freedom of responsible love, he does not pause to consider. The traditional pessimism, and the traditional allergy to every chiliasm, becomes a weapon with which he defends a supposedly unpolitical Christianity which surrenders with a mere shrug of the shoulders the evil world to "the most dreadful slavery," and regards as fanatical every quest for a better society, i.e., for a society in which material technical necessities do *not* lead to a loss of freedom. Granted, Wölber says rather later that he does not wish to call in question "the world's capacity for progress", but the redemption in Christ is for him so severed from society that the advocacy of "liberty, equality and fraternity" in his opinion has nothing to do with the Christian witness. For him the question "whether the centre of gravity of our message is the renewal of man or the renewal of the system" is one which "reaches so deep as to cause a schism in the faith". Thus he is clearly unable to understand that men who wish to serve the gospel for the regeneration of man cannot sever from this the regeneration of the system, because they see how masses of human beings are destroyed unregenerate by the system; because for the sake of "the regeneration of man" they wish to prevent the future age from being the "most dreadful slavery", and because they are alarmed by a situation in which his theology serves Wölber as a cushion on which he can take his ease.

The material necessity of technical development seems to make democracy impossible, if we understand by democracy the raising of the members of society to the status of Subjects (the latter term being used in a practical sense; for self-determination without free activity is a bad form of inwardness which must not be confused with the Christian inwardness of faith, which according to Luther is always expressed in action). A man is Subject in the social sense only if he can freely and actively help to determine the life and ways of society and thus realize himself socially. Emancipation of the masses by emancipation from the masses; this is the content of the concept of "responsible society," the content of democracy. The question is whether we should take a regretful leave of this ideal. Behind this question there stands another question: whether we really wish it at all, whether we have indeed ever really wished it. We are haunted by plenty of Superman theories, even in the heads of churchmen. It is indeed a trick of the pulpit to call every hearer to responsibility, but once outside the Church many of us go along with the crowd, which wishes to be led, and which can be glad if treated as an Object, as long as it is well catered for. This can be backed up by words of Luther, but is not made any more Christian on that account. It does not come so trippingly off our tongue when we note from the already cited quotations from sociologists that we too are going to be levelled down into these masses—Objects, unknowing or half-knowing—but in any case without responsibility and without a say in the hierarchical big business of our technocratic society. Then perhaps it no longer seems so easy for us to take leave of the democratic ideal, and we ask if we really must say farewell to it; we decide to offer a tough opposition, and so to fight for democracy now.

Here there is a disclosure of interests which underline this élitist thinking about the sub-personal character of the masses, and a disclosure of contradictions in the technocratic system which purports to be an attractive system for supplying needs. The "optimal efficiency" of function and productive power, of which Schelsky spoke, this productivity turned into a fetish, is indeed under capitalist conditions a productive power for profit, a maximum profit which has now admittedly become irrational. It is not a productive power answering the real needs of all the members of society.[8] Thus these needs are in no way better satisfied. If we like to talk about the "rising needs" of contemporary men, then this "rise" in efficiency means in reality that even the most primitive needs in modern civilization can be met only with much greater difficulty and more expense in money and in labour than in earlier centuries, and in many respects are much worse met, so that Sebastian Haffner spoke some years ago, in an excellent article, about our "falling standard of life". The profit principle, as a result of individual appropriation, hinders the utilization of the technically enhanced productive power of society for the better satisfaction of both the collective and individual needs of all the members of society. Only by these members themselves can these needs be ascertained through free consultations in social institutions, and given priority—in spite of the hindrances which the owners of the means of production create through their desire for profit, so long as the capitalist system lasts. But in a socialist system these needs can be given priority without such hindrances.[9] The incomplete satisfaction of needs; the inadequate development of the infrastructure (housing, health and education services, etc.); the inflationary tendency of prices; the squandering of money on armaments; advertising and the manipulation of artificial needs; and finally the exploitation and impoverishment of the Third World; all these phenomena, not only tend to the destruction of democracy but prevent technocratic capitalism from proving so satisfactory to the masses as Herbert Marcuse fears it may. "In the system of higher education, a wider range of curriculum, a larger number of institutions, and greater self-government are today fundamental requirements. The communication and culture media must be taken out of the hands of commercial interests. The place where democratic decisions are made must be multiplied and decentralized. Local and regional autonomy must be increased, and cultural institutions must be given the power of self-direction."[10] These requirements oblige everyone who, as Uppsala demanded, wishes to work for justice and human dignity in society to subject the phenomenon of high-power capitalism and technocracy to the most trenchant criticism, and to uncover the causes and interests which stand in the way of emancipation, without regard for our own interests which are involved.

I add some more quotations to help reflection and discrimination. The first is from Eugen Kogon, who has recently described "the mild 1984", with reference to West Germany. "Prosperity and military protection, that is the definition of the policy of the Federal Republic. Supplemented by 'regulations', it is also the definition of the future which has been planned for us—the mild '1984.' The tourists from abroad will find most things among us efficient and agreeable. It will only give concern to us the 'restless ones' the people 'whom nothing satisfies.' The refractory ones will be 'taken care of', all the others will be made to toe the line. If no public opposition is able to broaden the concept 'prosperity and military protection' into an all-embracing policy of peace and freedom, the democratic share in policy will be restricted to the reservations which individual members of the opposition in Parliament and in the country are already able to secure for it. Authoritarian practices will then become the normal thing in our life, without our usual standards being endangered—unless an economic crisis supervenes. On the contrary: anyone who obeys will be rewarded. Thousands of the older generation of our bureaucrats can hardly wait until this has been achieved."[11]

The next two both come from the already mentioned book of Ernest Mandel on the European Common Market:[12] "Either growing authority in business, economy and society; progressive curtailment of the last democratic rights and the last areas of individual self-determination, with an interplay of anarchy in the market economy and bureaucratic despotism, following on the growing tendency to plan our economy according to programme: or a resolution of the contradictions through socialistic planning, with the aim of answering needs, based on a really democratic centralized system of self-government by the workers."

"Contemporary technics, cybernetics, and atomic energy, require a consciously planned association of producers and consumers, based on free self-determination. Real economic democracy implies an economic system in which organization of the thrust of production, the guidance of investments, the hours of work, and the scale of restrictions on consumption required of every stratum in society, are decided by democratic discussion and by the mass of the interested parties themselves, and not behind their backs by a blind market, a dictatorial junta of business—and bank-magnates, or a supposedly omniscient politburo."

9

DEMOCRACY, CO-PARTNERSHIP, SOCIALISM

L'imagination au pouvoir! (Let imagination come to power!) This was what the French students wrote in May 1968 on the walls of the Sorbonne. André Dumas quoted this inscription in his enthralling address at Uppsala ("The Technological Possibilities and the Struggle for New Forms of Society") and defined imagination as "the agility of curiosity, conjoined with the realization of hope". Such imagination is really an indispensable virtue today for those who regard resignation and surrender as forbidden. It is to be opposed to *accedia*, indolence of heart of which Harvey Cox[1] says is "the decisive form of sin in our world today", and also, and perhaps principally, a political crime. Imagination must reach beyond and carry us beyond what today seems possible,[2] it must set an ultimate Utopian goal for our daily action, and thus keep the intermediate goals of this action from remaining accidental and without orientation. Without the Utopia of social democracy, that is, of socialism, even today the formal democracy which we still have can no longer be saved. It will be whittled away in the contradiction between the affirmation of emancipation and the fear of emancipation, between the interest in civic freedoms and the interest in their removal, which is peculiar to high-power capitalism.[3] "Privilege", according to Werner Hofmann,[4] is always to be defined as at once political and economic privilege, as "institutionally secured enjoyment of advantage by one part of society at the expense of another. Enjoyment of advantage has an economic significance; it means one-sided appropriation of part of the product of labour of others." Since in this age, under this technical development and these social circumstances, continually new possibilities for society, and consequently new temptations to exercise privilege come into being, privilege must be constantly attacked, exposed, and reduced, and forms of communal life that are free from privilege must be introduced.

The Church—A Brotherhood Free of Privilege

These forms of communal life ought not to be strange to the Church, which is indeed the privilege-free brotherhood in the world; for "the different offices in the Church give no justification for the privilege of some over others, but for the exercise of the service entrusted to the whole fellowship and required of it" (Barmen Declaration IV). If the Church speaks of the Lordship of God and the Lordship of Jesus Christ, it does not by so doing confirm feudal structures of privilege but undermines them. For not only is all human privilege thus limited (that is the anti-totalitarian effect of the Christian Confession), it is questioned about its function of service. This questioning aims at replacement of privilege by functions which in a purer fashion are only functions of service, no longer functions of privilege.[5] But the Church cannot be satisfied by giving effect to this only in its own life in contrast, as it were, to the world, and separating itself from the latter as something evil and irremediable. On the contrary, if it attempts to do this only in its own life, isolating itself from the surrounding world, then it will not succeed in doing so even in its own life. Instead, the modes of privilege of the surrounding world will exercise an influence on the Church also, so that in the end its free brotherhood will be only a matter of profession and feeling, that is, a matter of false inwardness. While in the empirical life of the Church, structures and persons will exercise privilege, and theory and practice will once again be torn asunder. Only if the life of the Christian fellowship influences the surrounding world—at least in tendency—will it resist the influence of the surrounding world upon itself. The Christian community is also "a fellowship of service in the world" because it realizes a privilege-free voluntary association, and thus serves the surrounding world as an example, encourages its members, who at the same time are members of society, and by experience stimulates their creative ideas and desire to participate in the destruction of privilege in the outside world as well.[6]

Co-Partnership—A Step in the Direction of Democracy

The Protestant Church is therefore doing nothing alien to its own nature when it takes up today the question of *co-partnership.* The primary importance of this question arises from the fact that, as the above quotations from sociologists showed, the authoritarian hierarchical structure of industry is not only an alien body in democratic society and in opposition to it, continually indoctrinating men in authoritarian and servile attitudes, but also because it serves as the source and model of the technocratic thrust against democracy. I have before me a paper drawn up by a Protestant study group, on which employees as well as employers were represented. It starts with statements which excellently describe the task of social institutions which is implied by the Christian message. It thus confirms the affinity between the Christian doctrine of man and democracy. "These institutions should help and encourage everyone to play his responsible part in the human fellowship in which he lives, and they should encourage him in the development of his human gifts." Further: "The interest in performance which men rightly expect of each other in the life of industry, must never supersede the obligation to respect each other mutually as thinking members of human society, who share responsibility for it." If this obligation is taken seriously and put into practice (the sketch proceeds to describe this principle in detail, and formulates a consensus of opinion reached among employers and employees), then a way is opened up for the workers in industrial firms to emerge from a situation in which they are treated as Objects (and are glad to be so treated, so long as they are taken care of in times of crisis by retaining employment and pay, and are treated kindly by employers and officials). They will then realize that they are themselves the bearers and moulders of social events. This will indeed require that the accounts should be entirely open to examination, and the limitations on co-partnership should be removed (and a better type of co-partnership should be devised than has hitherto prevailed in the Montan Industries[7]).

Co-Partnership and Socialism

What we are dealing with here is a *way*. The difference between the mutually contradictory interests of the workers and the owners is not reconciled by such co-operation and this should not be disguised, but publicly exposed, on the basis of their common interest in the efficiency of the business. Even by co-partnership, the fundamental contradictions of capitalistic production, with their harmful effect of which we spoke above, cannot be obviated but only the alleviation of their immediate consequences for the employees. The study which we mentioned, therefore, asks too much from the workers and all who are unable to regard the capitalist system as the last word, when it claims in conclusion: "Fruitful co-operation presupposes above everything else that an agreement has been reached about the fundamental characteristics of the economic system. If a considerable number of those representing the employees were to advocate an economic system in which private ownership of the means of production were to lose its function, or if the owners of capital were to call in question the fundamental equal right of the employees to partnership, or to aim at a disenfranchisement of the employees, this would make the co-operation in business which is the aim of co-partnership impossible. At most it would be conceivable in the form of an unstable co-existence of opposed interests for a limited period."[8]

All stability in the stream of history is only relative, and has its "limited period." A compromise like co-partnership can be relatively stable, until new conditions bring it to an end, even if during the period of its duration the participating partners have different aims. The one party seeks the maintenance of the present system, which they wish to make secure precisely by means of the compromise; the others the conquest of this system, and for them the compromise is a step on the way to this. To ask that the goal of a socialist society should be surrendered for the mess of pottage of co-partnership is to ask an impossible sacrifice. A compromise which has co-partnership as its condition must be resisted. Here it takes a chance as to how much socialist awareness there is among the workers at any one time. It can have become dormant and can reawaken. Above all the principal idea implicit in the sentences quoted must be rejected; that interest in socialism is confined to the workers, as a merely ideological expression of their immediate interests, which can also be satisfied in another way, e.g., by co-partnership; and that an owner of capital must automatically see his ideal in the preservation of the capitalist system. This would mean that both sides were limited to a narrow-minded standpoint directed by their interests, indeed their short-term interests. But the evil results of the capitalist system, as Marx always rightly insisted, injure the capitalist just as they do the worker, only in a different and not immediately material fashion. The insight may come to a representative of the employer class—and actualization may therefore be required of him—that better and juster systems are possible, and that in the long run his *human* interests and those of his children are better protected in a socialist society than in the present one. There are such employers who are able to see beyond their short-term interests and the ends of their own noses. It is neither in their power, nor in the power of the workers of our country to change our system at one blow. It has been one of the omissions of the Marxist theoreticians that they have not yet worked out a satisfactory theory for the transition to socialism in a highly developed industrial society, which is extremely sensitive to disturbance, in place of the old theory of revolution. It is certain that this transition cannot take place abruptly as it did in earlier civil wars. If it did it would be a heavy burden, not to be soon overcome, upon the socialist reconstruction. So there is actually a socialist interest in avoiding a form of transition that would be catastrophic, and it is just this that makes necessary a step-by-step "long march in the institutions", to quote a favourite saying of Rudi Dutschke. As such a step—as the introduction of those treated earlier as Objects to the status of Subjects, as the training of workers in the art of directing business, as a contribution to the introduction to democracy and the fight against anti-democratic tendencies—this is how co-partnership in industry is to be understood; and it is just in this sense that it can be advocated by a member of the employer class, if his ideas are up to date.[9]

The concluding sentences of the paper we have mentioned express an attitude which has the effect of distorting our judgment about events in the Third World. Our system, with its type of production, is unreflectingly regarded as the goal towards which the developing countries have to move, and by the attainment of which they are measured. If some of them decide for socialism, this decision is judged only according to how socialism is considered as a means fitted to bring them to the achievement of our status as a goal. Similarly the so-called liberalizing movements in the Eastern European states are often assessed only to see how far they aim at an approximation to the Western conception of freedom, which includes the bringing of the economy under the direction of private enterprise. The assumption is that they need liberation, but we do not. But we must reckon with the fact that socialism must not be understood merely as a means of emerging from the condition of under-development, but as a way *and* goal. It is not only a matter of the satisfaction of hunger, but of the creation of an emancipated and humane society. Value judgments about life in community which, though not entirely absent, are far from realization in Western countries, are given priority under socialism, and even if for the time being they are only on paper there they will not always remain so. But socialism presses on beyond state capitalism to a further stage, that of the creation of really socialist structures. Already the influence of the new conditions on habits of thought and attitude can be traced here and there: "Even occasional visitors to these countries are impressed by the social atmosphere which is created by the absence of the institutions of private property; another way of looking at things than that under the market economy."[10]

The Cybernetic Revolution and the Liberation of Labour

In these reflections—not from a motive of caution about predicting the future, but because I do not wish to go beyond contemporary problems—I have hitherto ignored one revolution which has already begun, and which is bound one day to overwhelm the contemporary distribution of property: the cybernetic revolution. Marx had predicted this effect of electric machines, because he could not imagine them as means of production in private hands. But he underestimated the many different ways in which it is possible to organize private property. Such organization can cope with every possible kind of machinery, even atomic reactors and cybernetic machines. However the really revolutionary thing about cybernetics is its incredible capacity of liberating human labour-power through automation. This liberation will not result in the creation of new reserve armies of the unemployed, for there will no longer be the kinds of work they can do. After a critical transitional phase of structural unemployment, whose burden must be carried by the whole of society—and for this the trade unions are already striving with far-sighted projects—mankind will for the first time in its history be confronted by the fact that the earlier ethic of productivity, which gave the individual his value in society, has lost its meaning.

In all previous societies the distribution of the social product was regulated according to the two standards of ownership and work performed. The class depended on the privileged status conferred by the first standard; in the past, socialism has removed the first standard and left only the second intact: "If any would not work, neither should he eat." This maxim from the Bible (2 Thess. 3: 10), was included by Stalin in the Soviet Constitution of 1936.

However, when automation has been developed to its greatest possible extent, work will be scarce and leisure plentiful, and the division of the ample production according to the criterion of work done would be so senseless as to compel the elimination of this criterion. An ethic which inculcated the obligation to work, and by work understood essentially only the alienated labour of production as a recompense for a livelihood, will have become obsolete. (Writers on theological ethics will do well to face this fact, seeing that most of them omitted to learn it from Marx in good time!) A team of American sociologists demonstrated some years ago that a thoroughgoing utilization of automation would so raise the productive capacity of the United States that even today—in a time when "A job for everyone" is one of the principal demands of Martin Luther King's followers and the Negro movement—it would be possible to replace the present mechanism of distribution by a new system, which would guarantee for every individual and every family an adequate income as their right, without demanding a *quid pro quo* of labour! "But the continuing linkage of income to labour has an important braking effect on the almost unlimited capacity of an automated system of production." This linkage is coupled with the other linkage of income to the private ownership of the means of production. Taken in conjunction, both of them are senseless, and if the second one were to be maintained, then it would mean a much more dictatorial domination by the possessors of the means of production over the non-property-owning masses than in any earlier class-society. The present system, which is built upon this possession, will not be able to survive. "Some day in the future it will be seen in retrospect that the sanctioning of a right to income (independent of productive labour), was only the first step in the reconstruction of the system of values of a society which was brought into existence by the three-fold revolution."[11] The contemporary socialist system will be more open to the consequences of automation, inasmuch as in their case only one of these "retarding influences," the linkage of income to work, is to be overcome, and not the other retarding influence of the privilege of possession. As far as I can see, while in our country previous discussions of the problems of the leisured society have neglected to study the viewpoint peculiar to each class-interest on full automation and the revolution it makes inevitable, one thing that has been made forcibly clear is that to be humane an automated society must be a socialist society. For this reason the affirmation of socialism by the cybernetic expert Karl Steinbruch is anything but accidental, and very far from being so "subjective" as he modestly expresses it.[12] "The subjective value-judgments which I here avow as my own, as highest priority for the health services, for education, for non-violence both in internal and external affairs, for equal educational opportunities for all, for social control of the production of necessary materials, of the sources of energy and the means of communication, for scientific and technical progress, are distinctive marks of socialism. It seems to be beyond doubt that in the age of perfected technics, and a crowded mass-society, no other form of society is in the long run capable of realization. The avowal of socialism is not a matter of metaphysics, but the insight that there is no other social structure which can in this age ensure that the work which must still be done by men and its emoluments should be shared out in a rational manner, and that the society should be a non-violent society in which the incredible weapons of power are not used for destruction. Certainly this Utopian socialism is different from what is often today described as socialism."

Automation and a Policy of Development

To date I have found only one indication of the significance of this glimpse into the future for the policy of development, and that is in the essay of a liberal American political economist, Robert Theobald, entitled "Poverty on the National and International Plane, a Storm-centre of Universal Crisis."[13] He asks whether it is really necessary for the developing countries first to pass through all the stages of the history of the industrial countries, with all their burdensome and painful cultural disturbance; the adoption of the Western labour and profit ethic.[14] "In my opinion the poor countries must make the transition from the era of an agricultural economy to the era of cybernetically controlled automation in one bound, without going through the detour of an industrial epoch." For if it is possible for them to go through such an epoch today, the education of specialists in automation is no less possible for them than the education of scientists and technicians for other types of industrial concern.

In the developed countries automation will have the effect that, once the profit-motive has become unnecessary, the motivation of the individual to further increase his income will lose its power. Instead, man will have to seek in other directions for the further development of his personal possibilities. His hitherto stunted talents for non-economic activity will at last get a chance of development. For the developing countries this would mean that as they faced the future they would with less interruption develop their traditional systems of values and the human possibilities immanent in them, and in this way enrich the rest of mankind, instead of first succumbing to a process of impoverishment in culture and the humanities through an industrial Europeanization, which involves the assumption that "work as such, or consumption at any price, is essential and determinative for the dignity of human personality or for human development".

Theobald concludes with the "minimum requirement." "We must create a new social system, if we wish to survive." For he is convinced that "the very nature of the framework of the present economic and social structure makes it impossible within that structure to overcome the principle of labour and consumption which is crippling man." He is, however, then content to complain about a "lack of good will," a complaint which is certainly justified. But it remains sentimental so long as no investigation is made into the causes of this lack; what conditions of the objective situation continually create bad will instead of good will in otherwise quite respectable Christian or liberal men, and what battle strategy is necessary to achieve the changes. Nor may Christians and churches believe, that when they have uttered heart-rendering complaints about the wickedness of men and the regrettable powerlessness of good will, they have done their part. The only thing that has value is an active contribution to change.

10

THE POWERLESSNESS OF CHRISTIANS AND A WAY OF OVERCOMING IT

These general remarks and suggestions about capitalism and socialism were certainly not intended to commit the Church to a socialist programme for society. The special meeting of the Synod of the Evangelical Church of West Berlin in June 1968 was right when it stated that, "We must at all costs avoid identifying the gospel with a political programme, and committing the Church to a particular party." But the same Synod affirmed not only the duty of individual Christians to exercise political responsibility, but also the obligation of the churches as corporate bodies to give *diakonia* in politics, and by so doing it was already taking the same line as Uppsala. These statements should only show that if the churches really become active in this direction, they must drop the blinkers they have worn hitherto, or else remain entangled in ineffectual moralization and declamation, and thus deceive both themselves and others. They will have to concern themselves with the problem of capitalism and socialism in a very different way from hitherto. They will not be permitted, as happened at Uppsala, to make general statements requiring changes of structure even in our countries, but must become clear, and make clear to others, what structures must be changed, and why. Without taking this risk they cannot even do their duty by the starving nations. "So long as a national political system does not rest upon social equality and economic justice at home—how can it be an instrument of international economic equality?" asked the Indian political economist S. L. Parmar in his address introducing the work of Section III at Uppsala.

But with this we ourselves are asked a profoundly difficult question. Who are we, to do all this? It is not only the consciousness of our powerlessness that threatens to paralyze us. What can appeals from the Church achieve? In the last months, in the United States, not even the experience of disastrous political murders, which shook the whole world, was able to break the lobby power of the National Rifle Association, and move Congress against them, to pass a reasonable firearms bill. How shall we be able to succeed against powerful interests which stand in the way of structural changes?

At Uppsala, at the end of his passionate speech (which perhaps for all that did not move the Assembly deeply enough) James Baldwin spoke accusingly of the power of the Church: "It has the power still, if it is prepared to do so, to alter the structure of South Africa. It has the power, if it is prepared to do so, to prevent the death of another Martin Luther King, Junior. It has the power, if it is prepared to do so, to compel my Government to stop the bombing of South-east Asia." Just a moment ago we were still convinced of our powerlessness, and now there comes a man who believes that the old Church, which has been dismissed as a mere ornamental façade, has power. Does he do it only to accuse us? But perhaps he is right in his belief and with his accusation. Perhaps our powerlessness is only an excuse. Perhaps we have more power than we believe; just at that point when our resolutions, passed unceasingly at synods and church conferences and delivered to the press agencies, become no longer the end of our consultations, but notification of our own action, the prelude to action.

Once more the young people can be a stimulus to us here. For a long time they too tried the way of resolutions. All at once they perceived that by doing so they played the game of a society which keeps the rules of the game because by so doing it secures itself against unwelcome changes. Then they broke these rules of the game. Then they became bad citizens and disagreeable. A new mentality spread among them, a new freedom. They set on one side the bourgeois respectability which toes the line and waits, and produces petitions. They are the children who openly say that in spite of his new clothes, the emperor is naked. A so-called new Eastern policy, a so-called university reform, a so-called protection of democracy for the time of crisis. Their laughter tears away the mask. Suddenly, the hollowness of the serious-minded, the mediocrity of the politicians, the hypocrisy of liberals, the corruption of prominent people can no longer be overlooked. They have thrown the authorities on the rubbish dump like old crockery, and that is why people are angry with them, and make every endeavour to go on as if nothing had happened.

They have discovered the unity of theory and practice. That is why they deride without sympathy the academic character of science. Every one of their discussions they guide along the way from thorough debate to resolutions about the next action. They are not content with having said something, nor are they even content with having done something. They are most self-distrustful. All this could be an excuse for not doing the necessary thing. They do not stop, they do not give up, they are always thinking of new ideas. They have no respect either for the rules of respectability or for the authorities. They are, in an enviable degree, without fear. That they are so few, are so far only a "small, radical, vocal minority", neither disheartens them nor makes them inactive. They do not wait for others, but begin themselves with what they wish to change; today with the critical university, tomorrow with a progressive kindergarten. To use the words of Daniel Cohn-Bendit,[1] they develop "a strategy of the active minority, which is, so to speak, a perpetual ferment" and, "the essential thing is to have an experience which breaks completely with the old society."

While we laugh at them with the arrogance and wisdom of age, does this last word remind us of something? Does it remind us of a time long past, two thousand years behind us, as our heroic legends tell the children, but speaking daily to us with their texts though covered deep in dust? The Christians too were once a "small radical minority", an "active minority", and for them too the essential thing was continually to have experiences in which they made a complete break with the old society. Only by so doing did they become a ferment, a leaven (Matthew 13: 33), against which the old society in vain resisted with brutal repression (until it hit upon the idea that integration and repressive tolerance are more successful!).

Someone may object that the movement of the young people has already begun to subside, that it will not last for long, and will also not achieve much. It may be so. According as we hope for this or fear it, we manifest who we ourselves are.

For anyone who sees the way of the compulsory society in East and West irresistibly travelling towards an entropy of "material necessity", this anti-authoritarian revolt spreading through every country can be an encouraging sign of hope. The one horror, the degeneration of the developed countries into the condition described in "1984"—the possibility of it began to lessen in a few years, and it is thinkable that the anti-authoritarian revolt may relax also the other devastating policies and tendencies. "The occasions of protest may be great or trivial; what is striking, and what causes a movement, is the epidemic conviction that real action is possible, where a moment ago it seemed as if nothing could be done."[2]

We can do something, only we must really mean business and have no fear, and refuse to give up, as indeed the Christian faith forbids us to do. But in this we must break the polite rules of the world we live in, we must fling out the banner as the young people have done; we must begin not with modest demands, but with radical ones. The far-ranging vision must draw the reality after it. Reality, as Hegel says, cannot resist when thought revolutionizes it. And we must not begin by seeking for the good will and agreement of the top people, the holders of privilege, but, following Mao Tse-tung's example, by beginning at the "grass roots," i.e., below, in our own circle, in the institutions we can reach, and in which we ourselves live. We must not set our hopes on the people in authority, nor yet on their replacement by others. A change in the personnel of the Establishment has customarily made less change than people had hoped. So long as the relationship between the Establishment and the lower levels remains the same, namely that of privilege and unaccountability of the top people, is guaranteed, the possession of privilege will continue to influence their attitude. One experiences this in the Church, not only in those who succumbed to *elephantiasis episcopalis* and *professoralis*, but even in those cases where the process of influence and accommodation takes effect more slowly and less obviously, but nonetheless disturbingly and paralyzingly. It is naturally not an inevitable process; there are people who resist it, but there are not very many of them, and even they are not quite able to nullify the ponderous inertia of the apparatus. Perhaps we can use the apparatus, we should utilize it as far as possible. But we cannot pin our hopes upon it. We must ourselves take the initiative, present *faits accomplis*, and also have the courage to throw a spanner in the works.

Who are "we"? It is to be hoped that the answer will be supplied by action. It is being given already. Where it is given it will be infectious like an epidemic. Should we here only look enviously at the young people, in whose case the solidarity of a generation is a contributory factor? Could we not instead understand their unrest and revolt as a part of that activity in which we too (both the older people and the Christians) ought to participate, and at the same time as an encouragement for what is our special task, a task in which we so much need encouragement? For there is nothing that so paralyzes and corrodes the Christian Church in its old age as the spirit of resignation. It hardly believes that it still has any kindling power. But one cannot at the same time be a Christian and give up hope. *Spiritus Sanctus non est scepticus* (Luther).

[1] *Neues Forum* (Vienna), March-April, 1968, pp. 171 ff.

[2] D. Bonhoeffer, *Letters and Papers from Prison*, London, 1960, p. 112.

[3] *Ibid.*, p. 85.

[4] K. Barth, *Christengemeinde und Bürgergemeinde*, 1946, p. 39.

[5] "The Exploding Church" in *The Observer*, London, 14 April 1968.

[6] *Uppsala Speaks*, Geneva, 1968, p. 13.

[7] On the political consequences of the Sacrament, cf. the sermon of Christoph Blumhardt "Das Abendmahl Gottes," on Luke 14: 16–24, in *Predigten und Andachten*, Vol. 3, 1928, pp. 387 ff. How suddenly relevant to our expenditure of Church moneys sound the sentences of Luther, which hitherto we have regarded as conditioned purely by their times! E.g. from his *Ninety-five Theses:* "Christians are to be taught that the man who gives to the poor and lends to the needy, does better than the man who buys indulgences" (43rd Thesis). "We should teach Christians that the man who sees another in need, and leaves him lying by the roadside, and instead spends his money on an indulgence, earns not the Pope's pardon, but the wrath of God" (45th Thesis). "St. Laurence declared that the poor were the treasure of the Church, but he meant the word in the (literal) sense of his times" (59th Thesis).

[8] *Europa, Gedanken eines Deutschen*, 1937, p. 14.

[9] Quoted from the African statesman Rabemananjarz in *Paqué, Africa antwortet Europa*, 1967, p. 143 f. Relevant to this whole section is K. H. Pfeffer's *Welt im Umbruch*, Gütersloh, 1966, Chapter VI, 1: "Die Christen unter dem Vorwurf der Rückschrittlichkeit."

[10] Compare the description of the two cities in F. Fanon's *Die Verdammten dieser Erde*, 1967, p. 30: "The area inhabited by the colonized subjects is not complementary to the area inhabited by their colonial masters. The two zones are in opposition to one another, and serve no higher unity. Dominated by a purely Aristotelian logic, they obey the principle of mutual exclusion. There is no possible reconciliation, each sees the other as having gone to extremes. The city of the colonial masters is a stable city, built wholly of stone and iron. It is a well-lit asphalt-paved city, whose dustbins are always full to overflowing with unknown, unseen, even undreamt of waste. The feet of the colonial masters are never visible, except perhaps by the seaside, but one never gets near enough to them to see. Their feet are protected by solid shoes, while the streets of their cities are clean, smooth without holes, without stones. The city of the colonial masters is a well-fed, lazy city, its stomach is always full of good things. The city of the colonial masters is a city of whites, of foreigners. The city of the colonized subjects, or at least the city of the natives, the Negro village, the Medina, the reservation, is a place of ill-repute, inhabited by people

of ill-repute. People are born there somewhere and somehow. People die there somehow, of some illness or other. It is a world without intervening spaces, people sit here on top of each other, the huts are on top of each other. The city of the colonized subjects is a starving city, starving for bread, meat, shoes, coal, light. The city of the colonized subjects is a city that crouches down, a city beaten to its knees, a city that slouches past. A city of Negroes, a city of Bicots. The look that the colonized subject casts at the city of the colonial masters is a look of lewd envy. He dreams of possession, all kinds of possession: to sit at the table of the colonial master, to sleep in the bed of the colonial master, if possible with his wife. The colonized subject is an envier. The colonial master is perfectly aware of this. If he unexpectedly catches that glance, he notes with bitter vigilance, "they want to take our place". That is true, there is no member of a subject race that does not dream, at least once a day, of establishing himself in the place of the colonial masters."

[11] *Ibid.*, p. 34.

[12] *Op. cit.*, pp. 20 ff.

NOTES ON CHAPTER 2 (Pages 11–17)

[1] Chr. Berg, *Die lautlose Massenvernichtung*. Berliner Reden 13, 1968, p. 15.

[2] R. Dickinson, *Richtshnur und Waage*, Geneva, 1968, pp. 71 ff.

[3] Thus J. Hamel in his address at the United Protestant Church Synod in Berlin-Babelsberg, February, 1968.

[4] *Church Dogmatics*, IV, 3, Part I, pp. 28–30.

[5] *Prognose*, *Utopie*, *Planung*., 1967, p. 21.

[6] See *Concilium*, 4, 1968 (6/7), pp. 403–411; see his book of collected writings, *Zur Theologie der Welt*, 1968, esp. Part III.

NOTES ON CHAPTER 3 (Pages 18–28)

[1] 1–4, *Uppsala Speaks*, World Council of Churches, Geneva, 1968, pp. 52–3.

[2] 5–8, *Ibid.*, pp. 48–9.

[3] 9–11, *Ibid.*, pp. 61–2, 70.

[4] In 1968, the Second U.N. Conference on Trade and Development was held at New Delhi. Its findings are contained in a report of the same title.

[5] The Conference on World Co-operation for Development, sponsored by the Roman Catholic Church and the World Council of Churches was held at Beirut in April, 1968. Its findings are contained in the *Report of the Conference on World Co-operation; Beirut*, 1968.

[6] Dr. Klaus Lefringhausen is a worker in the Institute of Social Science of the Evangelical Church of the Rhineland. He was present as an Adviser at Uppsala.

[7] On 20–25: Dickinson, *op. cit.*, pp. 80 ff.; "Appell an die Kirchen der Welt", *Dokumente der Weltkonferenz für Kirche und Gesellschaft*, 1967, pp. 138–144.

[8] "Politisierung—Gefahr für die Kirche", in *Evangelische Kommentare*, 1968 (3), pp. 136 ff. and 1968 (6), p. 329; on this, see E. Stammler, "Zwischen Politisierung und Neutralisierung", in *Evangelische Kommentare* 1, 1968 (7), pp. 389 ff. At the Hamburg Synod (May, 1968) the Bishop of Hamburg was seconded by the Hamburg Socialist party member Helmut Schmidt, who shared his concern for the National Church, opposing preachers "who drive the people away from the Church," and raised the "question whether people really ought to be permitted consciously and deliberately to propagate political ideology dressed up as theology, and under the cloak of the ministerial office, as is the case with this Theology of Revolution, which in fact seems only to be an attempt to clothe with a divine sanction their own world-view, their own sociology, their own political hopes and their own political opinions". (From "Theology and Politics; a Politician's Contribution to the Discussion", *Lutherische Monatshefte* 7, 1968 (6), pp. 277–280, passage quoted on p. 277). Here the aversion is based on a total conformity to the forces which have something to fear from revolutionary action. The challenge by the politician to the question of the legitimacy of Church involvement, is then seconded by the bishop on his side with a warning to the pastors that only if they keep strictly neutral in politics can the "contemporary field of social freedom" be preserved for the Church (together with religious education, Church tax, and the articles of the law against blasphemy), while if the preaching of disagreeable political sermons continues "the State will remove an essential basis on which our contemporary form of organization is established" (*op. cit.*, p. 141).

[9] As the Bishops' Conference of the United Evangelical and Lutheran Churches in Germany expressed it in their consultation of 10–11 May 1968 on "Church and Politics".

[10] Cf. the distinction drawn by H. Asmussen in his essay, "Das Heil und das Wohl" in *Evangelische-Lutherische Kirchenzeitung* 4, 1950, pp. 226–228, whose tendency is actually in the contrary direction. (As is often the case, Asmussen here has a political bias, which is not apparent, but is obvious in other places).

[11] Karl Barth, *Christengemeinde und Bürgergemeinde*, p. 26.

[12] In the Preface to *Hochschule in der Demokratie, Kritische Beiträge zur Erbschaft und Reform des deutschen Universitätswesens*, 1965.

[13] Thus I amend a statement of C. Fr. von Weizsäcker at an act of worship of the German Red Cross in the Pauluskirche in Frankfurt

on 23 June 1968, in case someone wishes to apply it in the case of the Church. "The neutrality of the Red Cross would not be believed in today if it were to neglect the task of preventing war, but no one, today or ever, would believe in its neutrality if it changed its policy and took sides." (*Deutsches Rotes Kreuz*, July 1968, p. 36). There are important analogies between the Church and the Red Cross; but the difference between the neutrality of the Red Cross laid down by treaty, and the freedom of the Church over against all political parties has recently been clearly illustrated in their different ways of acting in the matter of help for Biafra.

[14] An instructive example of this is provided by the essay of G. Schmolze, "Die Ueberparteilichkeit der Kirche. Die sozialpolitische Polemik in den Predigten Adolf Stöckers" in *Evangelische Theologie* 25, 1965 (7), pp. 370, 388.

[15] C. Fr. von Weizsäcker, "Hunger und Weltfrieden", in *Deutsches Allgemeines Sonntagsblatt*, 1968 (22).

[16] Similarity in the Report of Section III at Uppsala: "Powerful political lobbies are essential to create the necessary conditions. Trade unions, political parties and other forces which have been instruments of political and economic changes in the past in many developed nations do not show adequate concern for development today. The students and the intelligentsia can play a crucial role in the shaping of political opinion. The Christian community in many developed countries could be an effective force." (*Uppsala Speaks*, p. 49). And "the individual Christian is called . . . to make the issue of development a major factor in his electoral choice and in other political commitments" (*Ibid.*, p. 54). When members of parliament declare that the threat of such a use of the vote is blackmail, as one has heard some of them do in the case of the debate about the laws dealing with a state of emergency, they only show their strange conception of democracy. Of course they should be thus exposed to a pressure exerted by the electors, but in this case—in distinction from many other kinds of pressure—not against their conscience, but in support of their conscience.

NOTES ON CHAPTER 4 (Pages 29–33)

[1] See my book *Forderungen der Freiheit*, 1962, pp. 312 ff., where this question is discussed at length.

[2] Quoted by A. Biéler, "Gottes Gebot und der Hunger der Welt. Calvin, Prophet des industriellen Zeitalters," *Polis* 24, Zürich, 1966, p. 56.

NOTE ON CHAPTER 5 (Page 34–36)

[1] Quoted from *Neues Forum* (Vienna), January–February 1968, p. 42. In the "Law Concerning Development Aid Personnel" of the West

German Republic is stated (Paragraph 2, 1.3): "It is only possible to recognize as legitimate agents of development-aid schemes juristic persons under private law who undertake only to send development-aid workers to such schemes as are in agreement with the measures of assistance of the German Federal Republic." Such co-ordination with the political intentions of the federal government can only injure the free service of peace as disastrously as has happened recently in the case of the American Peace Corps.

NOTES ON CHAPTER 6 (Pages 37–58)

[1] On this point see the letters printed in *Kursbuch* 2, 1965, pp. 150 ff.

[2] K. Lefringhausen, *Fragen der Entwicklungsländer an die Industrienationen. Vorbereitungsmaterial für die Synode der Evangelische, Kirche der Union*, 1968: "But Western Europe, above all the former colonial powers, on which the others are structurally dependent, pursues within the framework of the Common Market a policy of autarky, and withdraws itself, as a rich men's club, into economic isolation, in order to prevent its own programme of production from being endangered by fluctuations in world trade." It is our mistake "that we have not systematically pursued the way of the European communities, and that we have left the fundamental ethical questions in the hands of the European 'technicians of integration'. . . . The countries of development would describe our previous lack of interest in European economic procedure as guilty, because just this policy of the European Common Market can mean death for countless human beings in the developing countries."

[3] C. Fr. von Weizsäcker, *Hunger und Weltfrieden*. (See Chapter 3, note 9.)

[4] The Swiss Protestant Church Council presented to the World Conference on Church and Society of 1966 the proposal that the Churches should try to ensure that in the rich countries, out of the seven per cent. of the national fiscal income, which the defence estimates on an average comprise, three per cent should be applied to development and considered as having been applied for the former purpose and therefore written off (cf. Biéler, *op. cit.*, pp. 57 ff., 80 ff.).

[5] See the memoranda, *Die Lage der Vertriebenen und das Verhältnis des deutschen Volkes zu seinem östlichen Nachbarn*, Hanover, 1965, and *Die Friedensausgaben der Deutschen*, Hanover, 1968.

[6] Von F. Baade, "Ost und West als Verbündete im Weltkampf gegen den Hunger", in *Stimme der Gemeinde*, 1968 (15/16), pp. 465–476.

[7] In the new *Internationale Dialog-Zeitschrift* 1, 1968 (3), which is concerned with the problems of development, the Hungarian J. Bognar, who is an expert on African affairs, claims (p. 264) that, "we cannot regard the development policy of both super-powers as on a par,

for while the political efforts of the Soviet Union aim at strengthening the tendency to freedom in the bloc, and national independence, the other super-power endeavours to create and elaborate new forms of dependence." He does not claim by this that the Soviet development policy is purely unselfish, but that it "makes a difference whether the country giving aid is directed by certain political considerations, or whether political conditions are laid down for the granting of credits. The first of these fundamental attitudes is realistic, and acceptable, so long as interests determine human action; but the second is unacceptable," for it "means political blackmail" when a state expressly couples its offer of aid with the condition that the receiver of this offer of aid must revise its foreign policy. Similarly J. de Santa Ana (who unfortunately was not present at Uppsala), in "Die wirtschaftliche Lage in der Dritten Welt und die Vorschläge für ihre Lösung." (Paper given at the Third Christian Peace Conference in Prague, March 1968), printed in *Stimme der Gemeinde* of 1 June 1968.

[8] I confine myself strictly to the share of guilt borne by the developed countries, and do not deal with the inalterable causes in the mentality, traditions and structure of the developing countries, because here we are dealing with only one question, what can and should be done on *our* side.

[9] For necessary enlightenment and proclamation in these days the voices of H. Kutter and L. Ragaz should be heard again in our Churches. (H. Kutter, *Sie müssen; Ein offenes Wort an die christliche Gesellschaft*, 1910; *Gerechtigkeit*, 1910, *Die Revolution des Christentums*, 1912) and L. Ragaz: (see the four Essays on him in the *Zeitschrift für Evangelische Elhik* 12, 1968 (4/5).

[10] On this the best thing is the essay by M. Barth "Marxisten und Christen im Gespräch" in the volume dedicated to this dialogue, Vol. 2/3 of *Evangelische Theologie* 28, 1968, pp. 73–107.

[11] And my interlocutor had forgotten what R. Bertram had said a few days before in his address to the whole assembly: "When the agenda which the world has a share in writing are the agenda of Jesus Christ our Lord, and when the Church's Pentecostal Spirit still gives courage, why should we not invite to the strategic councils of the Church also those secular men whose requests we have to take into account? And why should we ask for their advice only for the health services and social work? Have they not, sooner or later, an interest also in our evangelization and in the proclamation of the good news?"

[12] H. Böll, *Aufsätze, Kritiken, Reden*, 1967, p. 361. "It may be that Christianity has a bourgeois variant which I have never seen, although around me I see nothing but this variety." How close is the alliance between Christianity and the middle class and how much the resultant anti-communism is so taken for granted it is not even noticed, is seen

by the fact that expressions of this attitude of mind, by persons who advocate a non-political gospel and are vigilant supporters of the political neutrality of the Church, have never yet elicited a protest, although one comes across them every day. As a random selection from present-day reading material I may quote the Berlin *Tagesspiegel* of 18 August 1968: "Almost at the same moment it was recognized in Washington and Rome that the masses—above all in the Third World—would be driven into the arms of communism if they were not made, as in the United States and Western Europe, by a flexible capitalism, the partners of the employers." It cannot be denied that one could add to Rome the majority of Protestants. The exploitation of the Church for the preservation of the employers' society (a further selection from contemporary reading material) was recommended also to Federal Chancellor Adenauer by his friend, John Foster Dulles, in a correspondence at the end of 1955. It is true that the German Ambassador Krekeler then reported that he was forced to say to Dulles "that unfortunately in the Protestant Church as well as personalities of such transparent integrity as Bishops Dibelius and Lilje, and laymen like Herr von Thadden-Trieglaff, there was a whole group of clergy who had no realistic understanding of the problem of communism. I mentioned Pastor Niemöller in this connection." (Konrad Adenauer, *Erinnerungen*, 1955–59, Vol. III, 1967, p. 98). In considering our difficulties today in maintaining the unity of the Protestant Churches in Germany, we should never lose sight of the fact that because of this attitude the West German part of the Protestant Churches in Germany is incapable of achieving this task.

[13] The principal advocate of this view has been Walt W. Rostow, in his book *The Stages of Economic Growth*, 1960. It was represented at Uppsala by the English political economist Barbara Ward in a much applauded address on "Rich and Poor Nations." Similarly H. Besters in the evangelical and catholic handbook, *Entwicklungspolitik*, 1966, pp. 243 ff., 298, etc.

[14] On this see F. Vilmar, *Rüstung und Abrüstung im Spätkapitalismus*, 1965, esp. Chapter VI; in addition P. A. Baran, *Oekonomie des wirtschaftlichen Wachstums*, 1966; P. A. Baran, *Unterdrückung und Fortschritt*, 1966; P. M. Sweezy, *Theorie der kapitalistischen Entwicklung*, Cologne, 1959; M. Dobb, *Organisierter Kapitalismus*, 1966; P. A. Baran and P. M. Sweezy, *Monopolkapital*, 1967; C. Wright Mills, *The American Élite*, 1962. This thesis of Marxist authors is confirmed by the role which J. K. Galbraith in *The Modern Industrial Society*, Boston, 1967, ascribes to the military budget under contemporary capitalism. On the interest of a socialist system in as large a degree of disarmament as possible, and the conflict between this interest and the interest of a power-élite who have asserted their own independence in the Eastern European bloc, see Vilmar, *op. cit.*, pp. 60 ff., 253 ff.

[15] Since in the propaganda intended to awaken pity for such peoples as have fallen victim to communism, it is the custom to urge the limitation of freedom and equalization at a low standard of living as a principal argument against communism, it should be remembered that our historians are accustomed to praise the Prussian kings because they raised their state to greatness in a similar manner. We can call the communist military dictatorships in Asia the "Prussian phase" of these countries.

[16] P. Rieger, "0·62% Love of our Neighbour" in *Neues Forum* (Vienna), May 1968, p. 317. On the dictatorship phase in the life of such states the Report of Section III at Uppsala says (p. 48), "In some countries, as a result of widespread illiteracy, lack of adequate social consciousness and strong resistance of established power-structures to change, decisions on development may have to be made by a relatively small centralized group before a full democratic structure can be achieved. Such strategy can only be justified as an interim stage and to the extent that it shows its ability to promote development and enlarge the participation of the people". What is involved in such strategy may be indicated by a quotation from the instructive essay of George Büchner, Franz Deppe and H. Tjaden, "On the Theory of Social and Economic Emancipation of Developing Societies" in *Das Argument*, July 1965 (34), p. 31: "Effective economic development requires the transfer to the other sectors of the resources earned in the agrarian sector, with the purpose of providing income and sums for investment in these areas of the economy. This is an appropriation of resources in the primary sector which is not possible without possession of the land, and reforms dealing with land-utilization: it requires at least a diminution of the sector of unearned income of unproductive urban upper classes, the control of profits arising from both internal and in particular external trade, and also their transfer to productive expenditure. It demands, in the last place, the transfer of the profits of extracting industries and other exporting industries which are frequently still in foreign hands, to areas where they will advance the internal economic development. In this way the privileged economic status of the corresponding social strata, classes and groups, is at least diminished, if not annihilated, as is their privileged social status, through the mobilization, better education and rise in income of the hitherto unprivileged classes, which is demanded by the acceleration of economic development, and which might serve to broaden the possibilities of their political responsibility. Otherwise this whole development might have been compelled through the political enforcement of the economic claims of the poorer classes."

[17] This is most glaring in the case of China, cf. F. Greene, *Listen-Lügen-Lobbies. China im Zerrspiegel der öffentlichen Meinung*, 1966; G.

Amendt, *China—der deutschen Presse Märchenland,* Voltaire-Flugschrift 13, 1968.

[18] Even the latest movement in Czechoslovakia has shown that the attraction of the capitalist system is only a limited one; the retention of the socialist system in Czechoslovakia is not motivated merely by caution in matters of foreign policy, but is based on the will of the people. It is just this which is decisive for the condemnation of the Soviet occupation.

[19] The imposition of communism on the East European countries and on East Germany after the Second World War by the Soviet Army cannot be put forward as a refutation of this. It resulted from the Soviet Union's need of security, and from the brutality of Stalinist policy. But in our context we are dealing with the problems of the Third World, in which the Soviet Union cannot apply the methods of that time, nor, as has become evident in the meantime, does it wish to apply them.

[20] *Op. cit.*, p. 48.

[21] *Christen plündern Christen* (see Chapter 1, note 1).

[22] Cf. H. E. Bahr, "Kirchen als Träger der Revolution. Ein politisches Handlungsmodell am Beispiel der U.S.A.", *Konkretionen* 3, 1968.

NOTES ON CHAPTER 7 (Pages 59–65)

[1] T. Rendtorff and H. Tödt, *Theologie der Revolution. Analysen und Materialien*, 1968; C. E. Braaten, "Theologie der Revolution" in *Lutherische Monatshefte* 7, 1968 (5), pp. 215–220; Chr. Walther, "Theologie der Revolution" in *Lutherische Monatshefte* 7, 1968, pp. 221–224.

[2] The first shot was fired by R. Shaull with his book *Encounter with Revolution*, 1963; then followed in 1964 his essay "Revolution in theologischer Perspektive," in Rendtorff and Tödt, *op. cit.*, pp. 117–139, in preparation for the Geneva Conference of 1966, and his address there: "Die revolutionäre Herausforderung an Kirche und Gesellschaft," in *Appell an die Kirchen*, pp. 91–99, and Shaull's contribution in C. Oglesby and R. Shaull's *Containment and Change*, New York, 1967. Compare also the report of the Theological Commission of the Christian Peace Conference (Sofia, October 1966): "Theologische Besinnung über die Revolution," in *Junge Kirche* 27, 1966, pp. 65 ff. A Consultation of the World Council in Zagorsk (March 1968) produced an important contribution, see: *Oekumenische Diskussion* IV, 1968 (2), pp. 80–84. On the whole question compare number 27 of *Evangelische Theologie* devoted to the theological problem of revolution, 1967 (12), together with J. Moltmann's address delivered at Marienbad, "Die Revolution der Freiheit", Volume II of the same year (now in *Perspektiven der Theologie. Gesammelte Aufsätze*, 1968, pp. 189–211). See also Moltmann's essay "Existenzgeschichte und Weltgeschichte. Auf dem Wege zu einer politischen Hermeneutik des

Evangeliums," in *Evangelische Kommentare* 1, 1968, pp. 13–20 (now in *Perspektiven*, pp. 128–145); and lastly my theses "Die Revolution des Reiches Gottes und die Gesellschaft," which appear in the volume of collected essays: P. Neuenzeit, ed., *Die Funktion der Theologie in Kirche und Gesellschaft*, 1969.

[3] "Revolutionary atheism and Christian conservatism in their mutual opposition confirm the incompatibility of revolution and Christian faith." B. Wielenga, "*Meditation* über Europa's revolutionäre Tradition," in *Junge Kirche* 27, 1966 (p. 135). We would gladly learn how H.-O. Wölber finds in the Old Testament Covenant-Promise together with the Ten Commandments, and in the Pauline language about the "Fruits of the Spirit" not only "a characteristic controlling the character of the expected revolution" (that is right), but also a "profoundly anti-revolutionary character". What kind of one-sided concept of revolution, and what kind of one-sided concept of grace, is here presupposed; a concept which condemns man to passivity?

[4] Cf. also his book *Asien und seine Christen in der Revolution, Th. Exh.* 145, 1968.

[5] Instead of this, people are prepared, in their rejection of revolution, to forget the assumptions they are prepared to make in the case of war. An example of this is provided by Vilmos Vajta's comments in the good volume of the *Lutherischen Rundschau* on *Menschenrechte, 1948–1968* (July 1968), in which he writes (pp. 267 ff.): "Injustice cannot be fought by injustice, because this only adds fuel to the fire. Only the man who does not admit the common guilt of humanity, and does not accuse himself, can be the captive of the delusion that human rights could be vindicated through revolt and revolution". Vajta equates revolution with "hate-filled injustice", and asks, "can then recognition be won for the human rights which are today in extreme peril in many parts of the world, through the injustice which is a phenomenon accompanying all armed revolutions?" He himself reminds us of the repudiation customary today of the doctrine of the "just war," but if his argument is to hold water, then he would at the same time have to repudiate along with revolution every kind of armed vindication of justice in this world, the army, police and the law courts, since these things are never unaccompanied by the phenomenon of injustice. But this as a Lutheran he cannot be ready to do. Thus this argument against revolution is ideological and not theological.

[6] It is not possible to make a legitimate objective statement without considering the historical context of a biblical text. Concerning such matters see K. Steinbuch, *Falsch Programmiert*, 1968, p. 58. "What shall we do with the text 'be fruitful and multiply and fill the earth' in an age of over population and world-wide hunger? What about the praise of work in an age of increasing automisation? and what of obedience over against authority in times when only resistance is moral?"

[7] *Uppsala Speaks*, p. 67.

[8] Quoted from H. Thimme's address "Kirche und sozialer Weltfriede" delivered at the German United Protestant Church Synod, February 1968.

[9] Compare the soundtracks of such trials in Heynowski and Scheumann's *Piloten im Pyjama*, East Berlin, 1968; also J. Takman, *Napalm*, East Berlin, 1968, and the collection of American press reports published by American Christians and Church representatives about the infringements of international law in the conduct of war by American troops in Vietnam: *In the Name of America*, Annandale, Virginia, 1968.

[10] Quoted in *Junge Kirche* 29, 1968 (7), p. 439.

NOTES ON CHAPTER 8 (Pages 66–79)

[1] Karl Lefringhausen, *op. cit.*, p. 4 (see Chapter 6, note 2).

[2] Compare with what follows the excellent interpretation of the student revolt by F. Marquardt, *Studenten im Protest*, 1968.

[3] On this point: *Wider die Untertanenfabrik, Handbuch zur Demokratisierung der Hochschule*, St. Leibfried, 1967; also, *Die angepasste Universität*, suhrkamp edition 265, 1968; earlier, W. Nitsch, U. Gerhardt, C. Offe, and U.K. Preuss (see Chapter 3, note 6).

[4] These quotations from H. Schelsky, E. Voegelin, and H. P. Bahrdt respectively, come from the essay by J. Miehe, "Nachtrag zur Technokratie-Debatte" in *Atomzeitalter*, 1968 (1/2), pp. 65–70.

[5] For Voegelin's vision of a great industrial structure embracing the whole of society is indeed unrealistic under capitalist conditions, in so far as it does not imply a national society which then would be only a preliminary to the great industrial structure embracing the whole of mankind. In the vision, capitalism turns into a kind of socialism, but of the perverted Stalinist type which novels about the future, like Orwell's *1984*, have depicted. The socialism of which I am speaking in this book of mine, is precisely the alternative to this technocratic vision; this, however, reveals the "material compulsion" of a type of thinking which can only associate technology with an authoritative structure of society, because of its deep abhorrence of a socialist democracy in which the privileges of the bourgeois society are removed.

[6] Thus E. Mandel, *Die EWG und die Konkurrenz Europa-Amerika*, 1968, p. 109, following the French political economist Ph. J. Parber.

[7] *Op. cit.*

[8] The classical theory of capitalism, given a new lease of life by neo-liberalism, claimed that these needs are ascertained and satisfied by the free market. But this was always true only of the needs for private consumer goods, not for the collective needs (air travel, transport, education, recreation, amenities, etc.) which never had a

square deal. In addition, the former type of needs is increasingly subject to manipulation, and in the second category the freedom of the market, and consequently the influence of the consumer, is increasingly whittled away in monopoly capitalism. Not even as consumer is man a subject.

[9] On the problem of needs, cf. A. Gorz, *Zur Strategie der Arbeiterbewegung im Neokapitalismus*, 1967 (esp. Ch. III "Ziel und Zweck der Arbeit"; Ch. IV, "Das Konsummodell") also E. Mandel, *Marxistische Wirtschaftstheorie*, 1968.

[10] A. Gorz, *ibid.*, p. 162.

[11] Quoted from the *Bulletin des Fränkischen Kreises*, April 1968.

[12] (See note 6 of this Chapter.) *Die EWG*, pp. 106, 107.

NOTES ON CHAPTER 9 (Pages 80–89)

[1] *Der Christ als Rebell*, 1967, pp. 32 ff.

[2] At Uppsala the cabaret artist Hans-Dieter Hüsch appeared at the Ecumenical Cafe Chantant with songs whose words were worth the attention of the participants. One of them ran thus (quoted with thanks for his permission):

WHAT IS TAKEN FOR GRANTED

There were times
When what is taken for granted today
Was not taken for granted.
This justifies us in assuming
That what is not taken for granted today,
Will one day be taken for granted.

But who has made what was not taken for granted
In the course of time to be taken for granted?

Spinners of dreams, madmen, juvenile delinquents, utopians,
Outsiders, lone wolves, workers and dreamers;
All of them suspect elements.

But who is it that makes what should be taken for granted
Not be taken for granted?

The middle-men,
Who are fed from the breadcrumbs
That fall from the President's table,
And then say:
I had lunch with the President yesterday,
He is such a simple man,
He gives himself absolutely no airs,
You would hardly think that he is a President . . . .

But one day,
When what is not taken for granted today
Will be taken for granted,
The middle-men will even be keen
To sell the President to the people.

But the people will then take no notice of them,
Because then it will be taken for granted
That no one takes notice of them.

And friends, I ask you to ponder this
The world has not yet been thought through,
There is no peace or freedom yet,
Only struggle and fighting for money, and greed
For monopoly and power.

Humanity is still only a dream on paper!
And every evening in our self-satisfaction,
We wish each other goodnight.

[3] More details about this in J. Agnoli, *Die Transformation der Demokratie*, 1967, and in *Neue Kritik*, April 1968.

[4] *Stalinismus und Antikommunismus*, 1967, p. 130.

[5] This seems to have been the impulse of Schleiermacher's theological thinking about politics, as it has now been depicted by Y. Spiegel, *Theologie der bürgerlichen Gesellschaft. Sozialphilosophie und Glaubenslehre bei F. Schleiermacher*, 1968. Spiegel's work ends with the sentence, "He faced quite frankly the consequence that when political authority no longer rests on the will of the monarch, but on the consensus of the people, even the authority of God can only be expressed and understood through the medium of democratic persuasion."

[6] This is the way that Karl Barth (*Christengemeinde und Bürgergemeinde*) has described the service of the Christian community to society. Our experience has since confirmed how right he was, when as early as 1938 (in his book *Rechtfertigung und Recht*), to the astonishment of many German theologians, he put forward the thesis of the "affinity" of the Christian Church with the democratic state.

[7] (*Eine Schweizer Stimme*, Zürich, 1945, p. 53). The question of co-determination is at present much discussed in Germany. A type of such co-determination is already to be found in the Montan-Union Industries (a supra-national combine of mines and steelworks in West Germany, France and the Benelux Countries). Here the trade unions contribute the same number of representatives to the supervisory council as do the shareholders, and in addition to these two equal groups there is a neutral member of the council. Further, the trade unions send a member—the so-called employee director—to the board of directors. Now it is planned that this model should be followed by all

the greater industrial concerns, whether in the same, or in a different form, is still the matter of lively discussion. The Socialist Party of Germany (S.P.D.) supports this proposal, while the Christian Democratic Union (C.D.U.) is opposed to it. At the moment this is one of the most important points of discussion in the internal politics of West Germany.

[8] The sentences quoted are noteworthy evidence of the decisive importance of the ownership of the means of production even today. The legend that this thesis of Marx is out of date because today the control of poverty is exercised in many ways, and is also limited by the intervention of the state in the economy, and by means of the managerial class, is actually put about by the parties who by their interest in such statements confirm the abiding validity of the Marxist thesis. For had the property become a matter of no interest, then there would be no need to trouble about it, and it would be possible with greater freedom to contemplate with others the transition to socialism. Cf. Mandel, *Die EWG*, p. 100: "In no case is economic power exercised by 'fellows without property.' This is known also by the so-called managers, whose whole effort is aimed at the quick acquisition . . . of great wealth."

[9] That for this reason the democratization of the universities by means of types of co-partnership there and the so-called mediating structures, is supported by me, must be evident.

[10] N. Birnbaum, "Die Krise marxistischer Soziologie," in *Frankfurter Hefte*, 1948 (4), p. 24.

[11] Memorandum. By the three revolutions are meant the cybernetic revolution, the revolution in the technology of arms, and the spiritual revolution caused by the dissemination of the idea of human rights.

[12] *Op. cit.*, p. 155. On the ambivalent possibilities of automation for democracy and technocracy; cf. B. Nirumand and E. Siepmann, "Die Zukunft der Revolution," in *Kursbuch* 14, 1968, pp. 71–79.

[13] *Internationale Dialog-Zeitschrift* 1, 1968 (3), pp. 246–255.

[14] This challenge is issued with the utmost assurance and regarded as inescapable. But it is the expression of a sublimely arrogant colonialism, as is shown by the essay of R. Panikkar, "The European Tradition and the Renascent World," in *Communio Viatorum* XI (Prague), 1968 (1/2), pp. 9–20.

NOTES ON CHAPTER 10 (Pages 90–94)

[1] In his conversation with J. P. Sartre, *Die Zeit*, 31 May 1968.

[2] So Paul Goodman, "In praise of Populism," in *Commentary* (New York), June 1968, p. 25. I am sorry that I cannot append to this book Paul Goodman's speech to the members of the United States Armament Industry in October 1967, but must content myself with referring my readers to it "An hour's chat with the Armament Industry", *Kursbuch* 14, 1968, pp. 33–44.